SAFELY ENDANGERED comics

SAFELY ENDANGERED COMICS

CHRIS McCOY

Andrews McMeel
PUBLISHING®

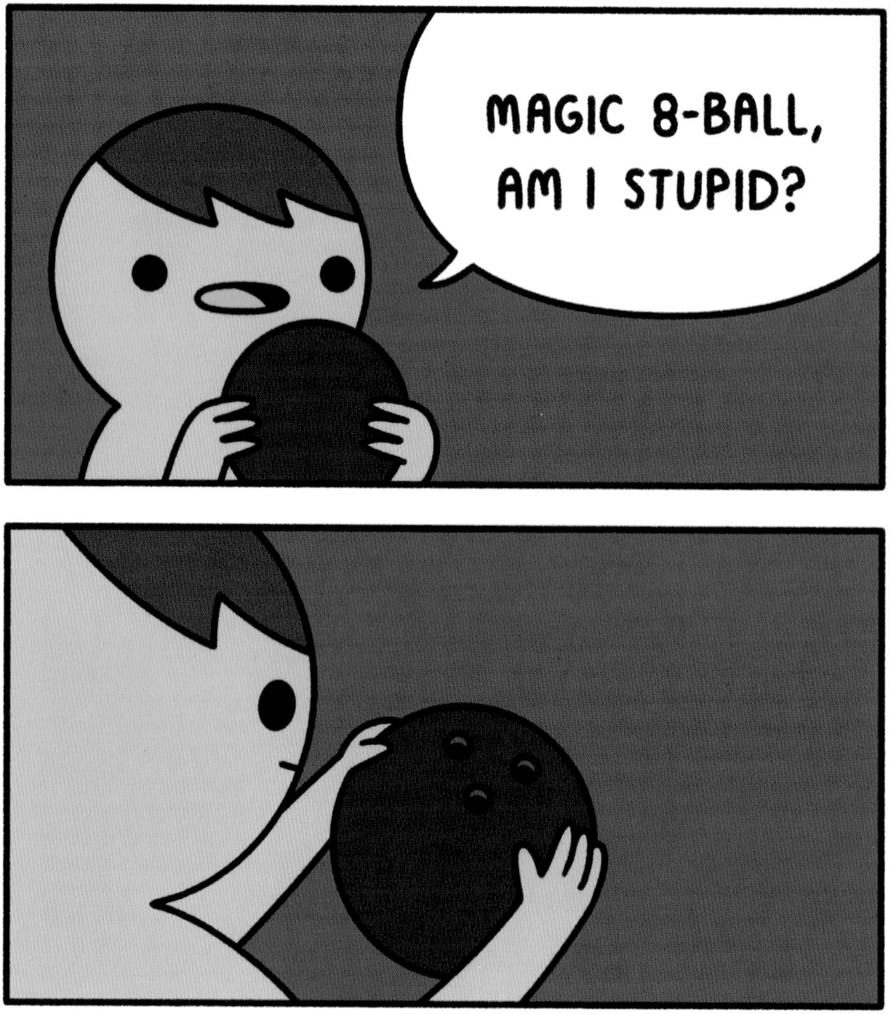
MAGIC 8-BALL, AM I STUPID?

YOUR PROSTATE FEELS HEALTHY
THANKS, DOCTOR
DOCTOR?

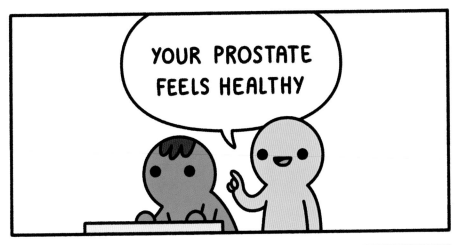

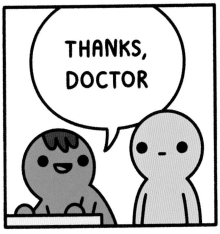

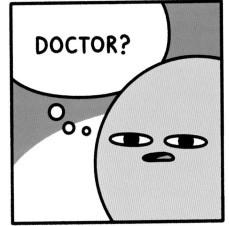

F
AMY
JUST BEEN STABBED. WERE IS THE NEAREST HOSPITAL??
LIKE COMMENT
WRITE A COMMENT...
TAP
TAP
AMY
JUST BEEN STABBED. WERE IS THE NEAREST HOSPITAL??
LIKE COMMENT
BILL WHERE*
WRITE A COMMENT...

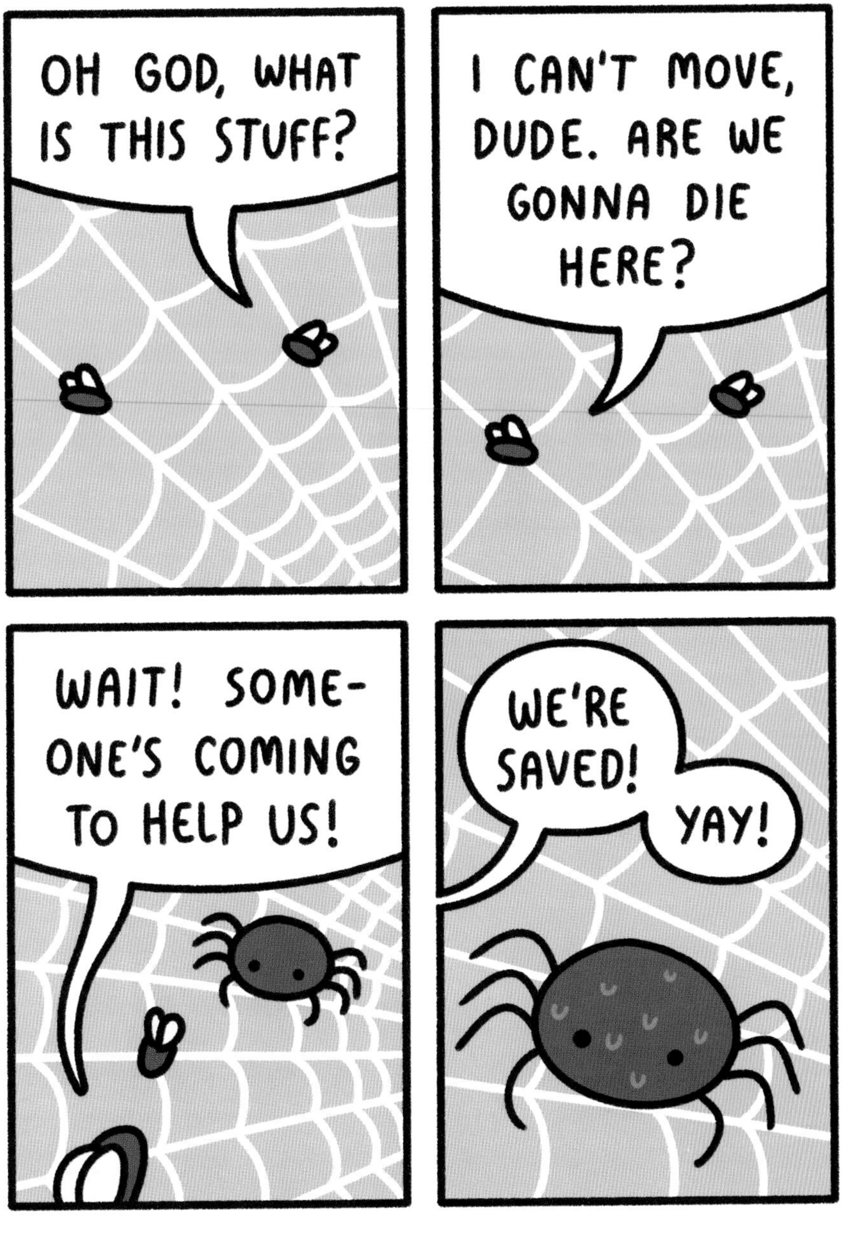
OH GOD, WHAT IS THIS STUFF?
I CAN'T MOVE, DUDE. ARE WE GONNA DIE HERE?
WAIT! SOME-ONE'S COMING TO HELP US!
WE'RE SAVED!
YAY!

STAY-AT-HOME SUPERHEROES

BATH MAN

IRONING MAN

INCREDIBLE SULK

SNACK PANTHER

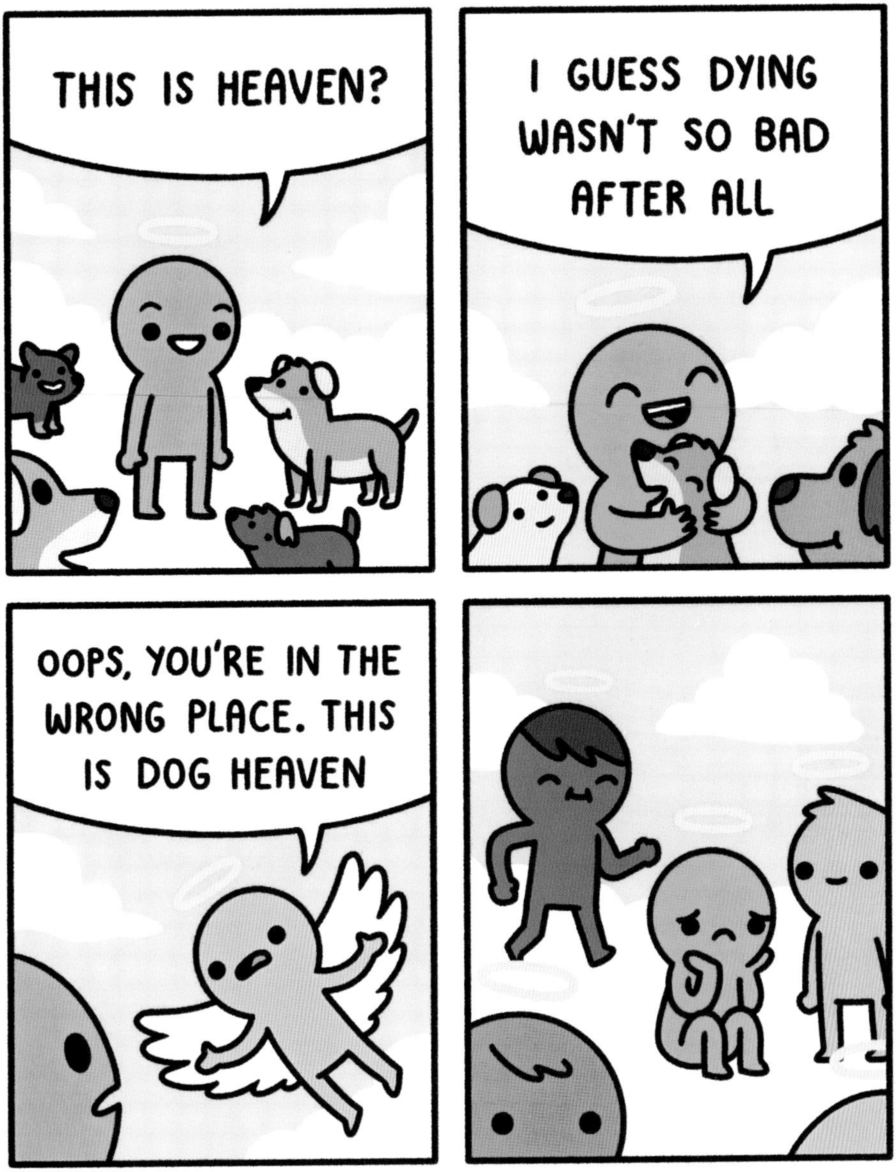
THIS IS HEAVEN?
I GUESS DYING WASN'T SO BAD AFTER ALL
OOPS, YOU'RE IN THE WRONG PLACE. THIS IS DOG HEAVEN

NOO!
BILLY!
WEEE!
HE WAS MY BEST FRIEND
WAIT GUYS... BILLY'S BACK!
THE BILLY YOU KNOW IS DEAD
MY NAME IS WILLIAM

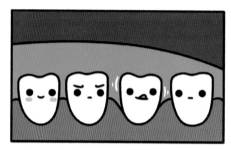

GYM
HEY, MOVE IT JACKASS
YOU'RE ON MY MACHINE

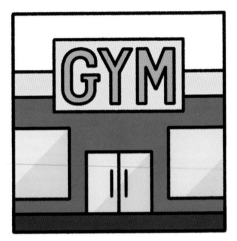

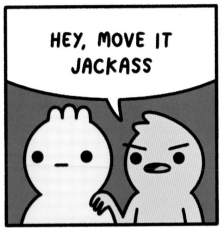

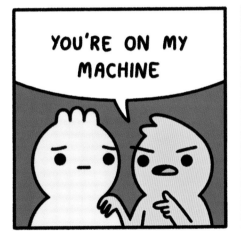

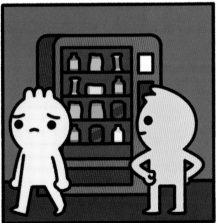

SHIT

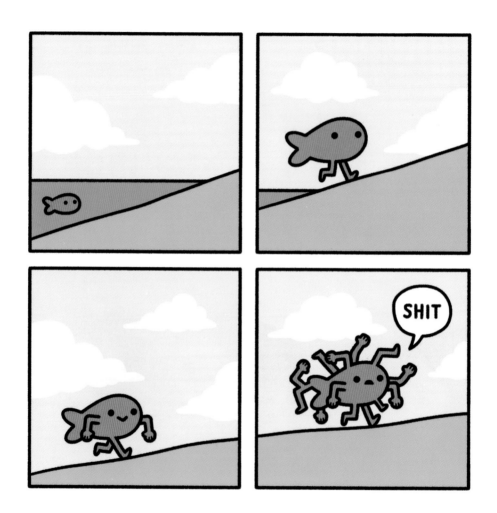

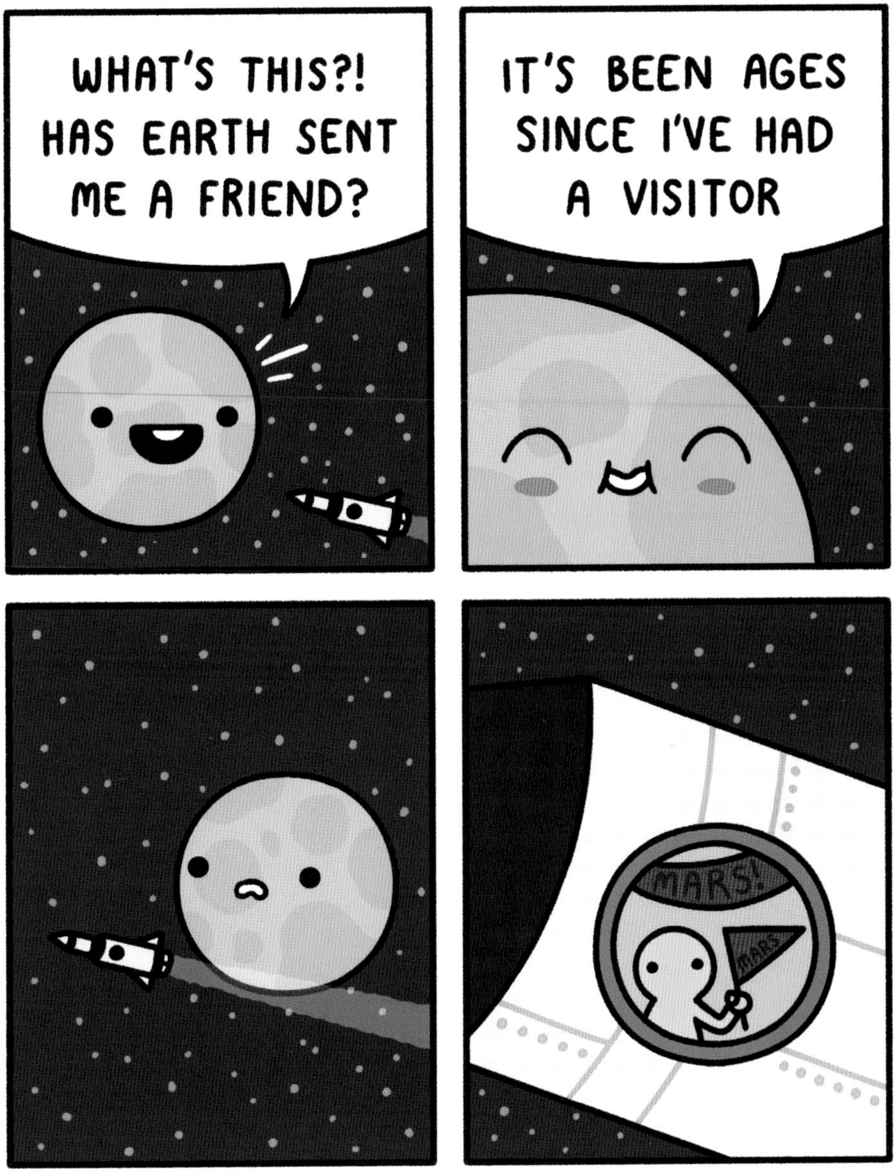
WHAT'S THIS?! HAS EARTH SENT ME A FRIEND?
IT'S BEEN AGES SINCE I'VE HAD A VISITOR
MARS!
MARS

YOU LOOK TIRED
I'LL SLEEP WHEN I'M DEAD
YEARS LATER
FASTER
GOD DAMMIT

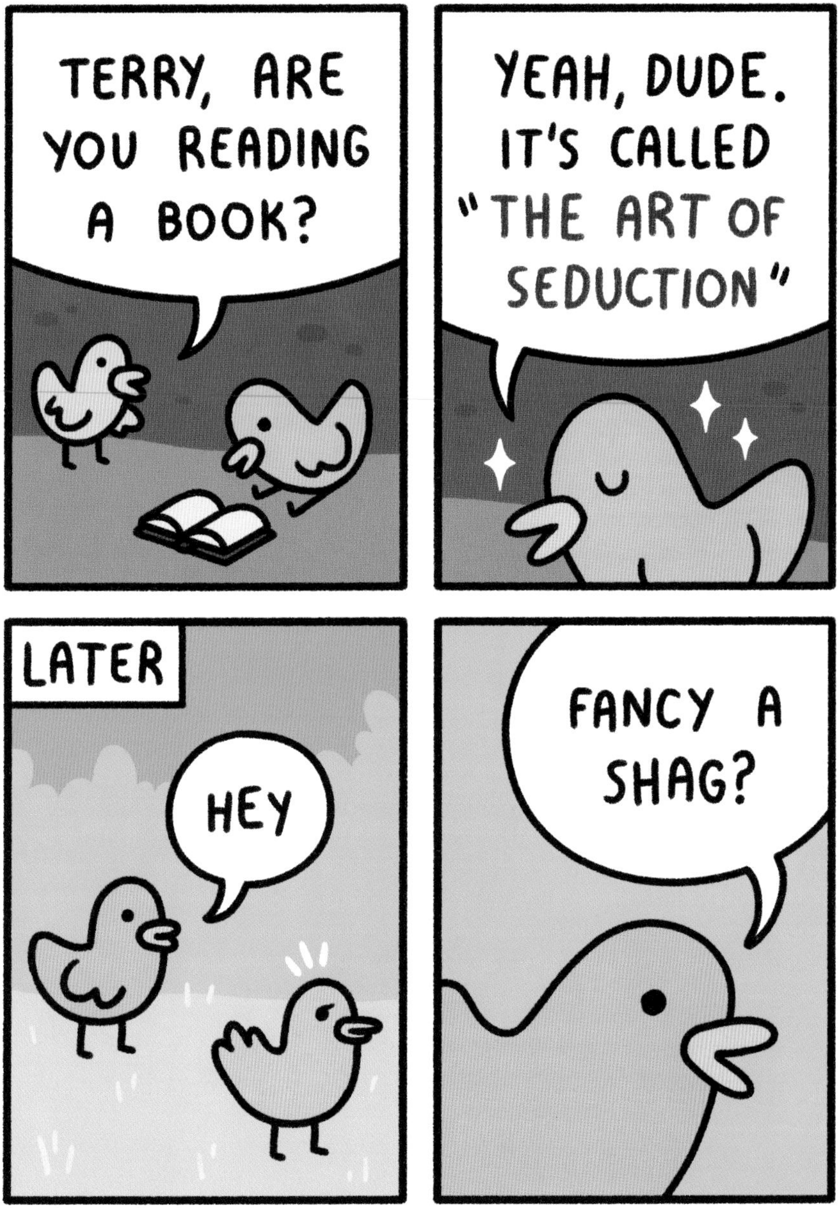
TERRY, ARE YOU READING A BOOK?
YEAH, DUDE. IT'S CALLED "THE ART OF SEDUCTION"
LATER
HEY
FANCY A SHAG?

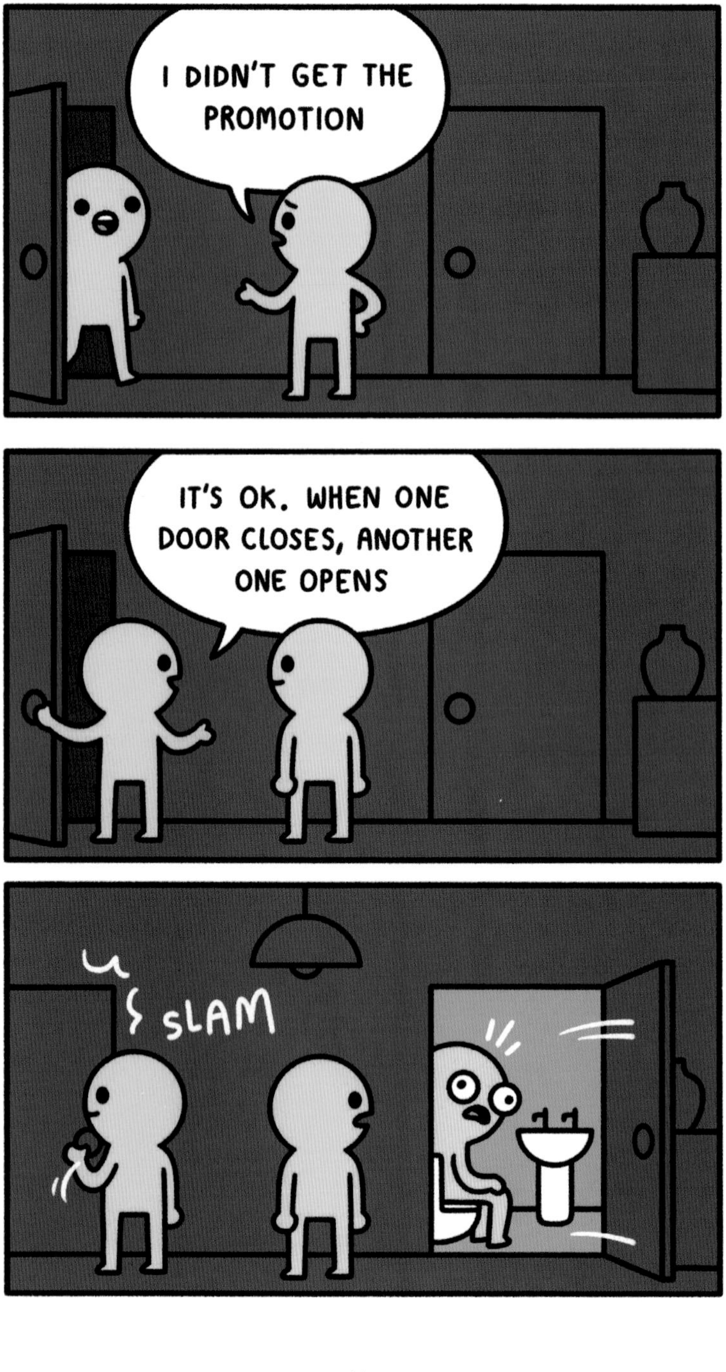
I DIDN'T GET THE PROMOTION
IT'S OK. WHEN ONE DOOR CLOSES, ANOTHER ONE OPENS
SLAM

HOW TO SEND A TEXT IF YOU'RE A GRIZZLY BEAR

1. ATTEMPT TO GRIP THE PHONE WITH YOUR HANDS

2. REALISE YOU HAVE STUPID BEAR PAWS

3. MAUL NEAREST HUMAN

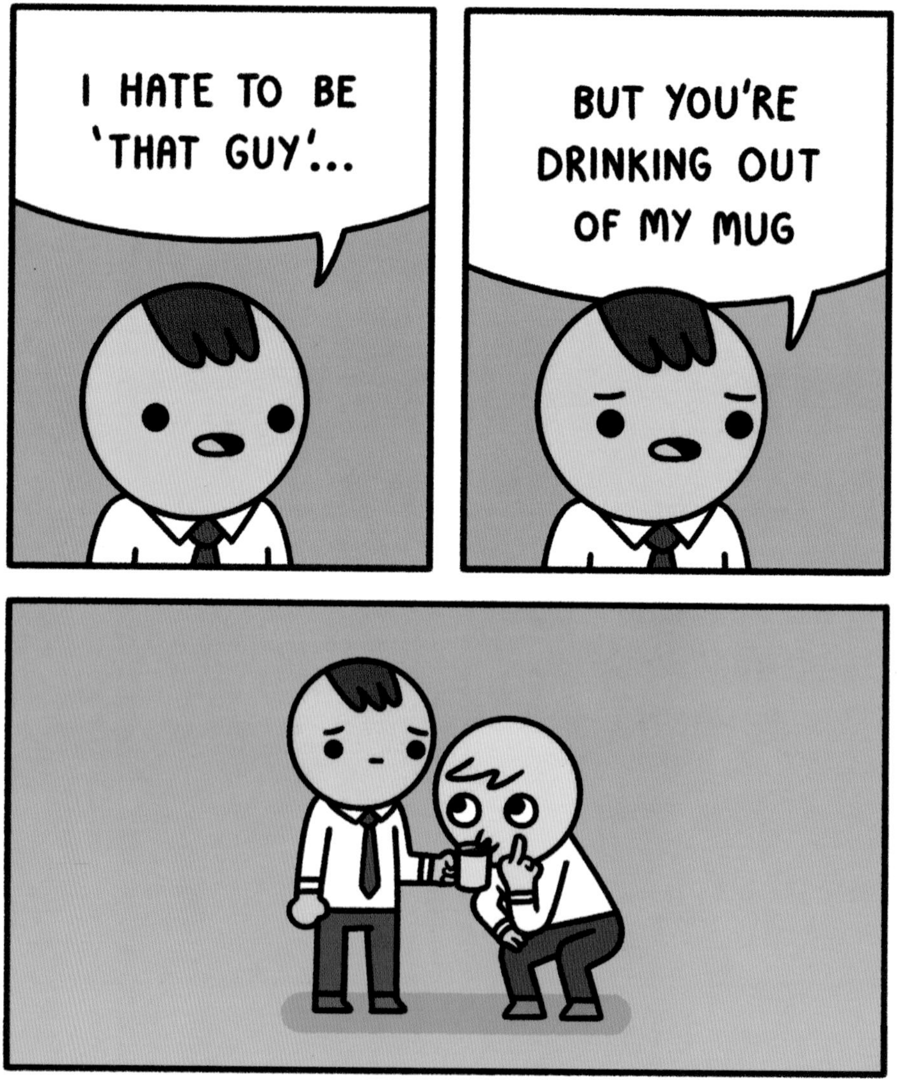
I HATE TO BE 'THAT GUY'...
BUT YOU'RE DRINKING OUT OF MY MUG

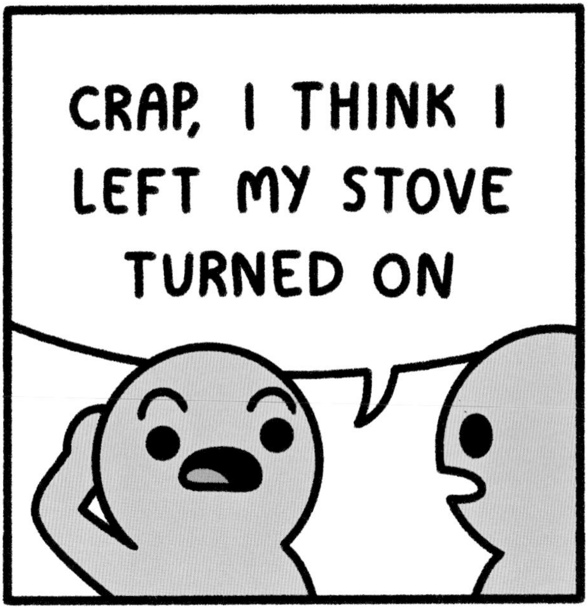
CRAP, I THINK I LEFT MY STOVE TURNED ON

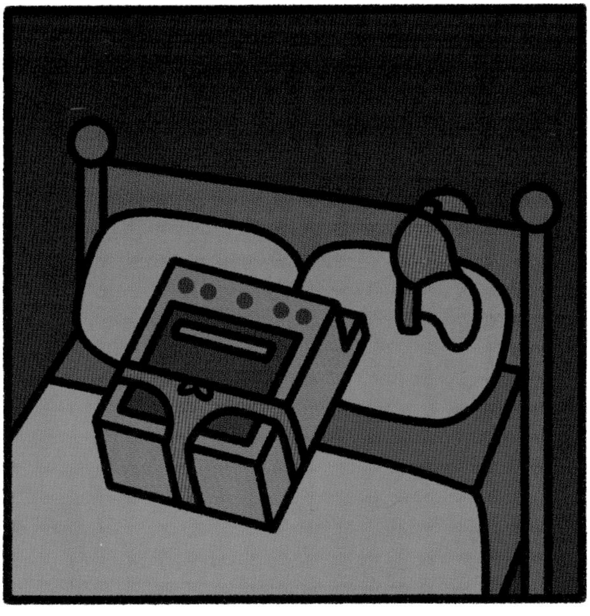

I WISH I WAS RICH
SON OF A...
VALUABLE COIN DISCOVERED IN FOUNTAIN
MORE ON PAGE 6

OMG, THAT DOG IS SO SAD
SAD DOG GOES VIRAL!
SAD DOG, WHY ARE YOU SO SAD?
THIS IS JUST HOW MY FACE IS

TODAY, I'M GONNA SAY HELLO TO MY HERO

OMG, HE'S RIGHT THERE!

CELEBRATION AS ROCKET DESTROYS DEADLY ASTEROID

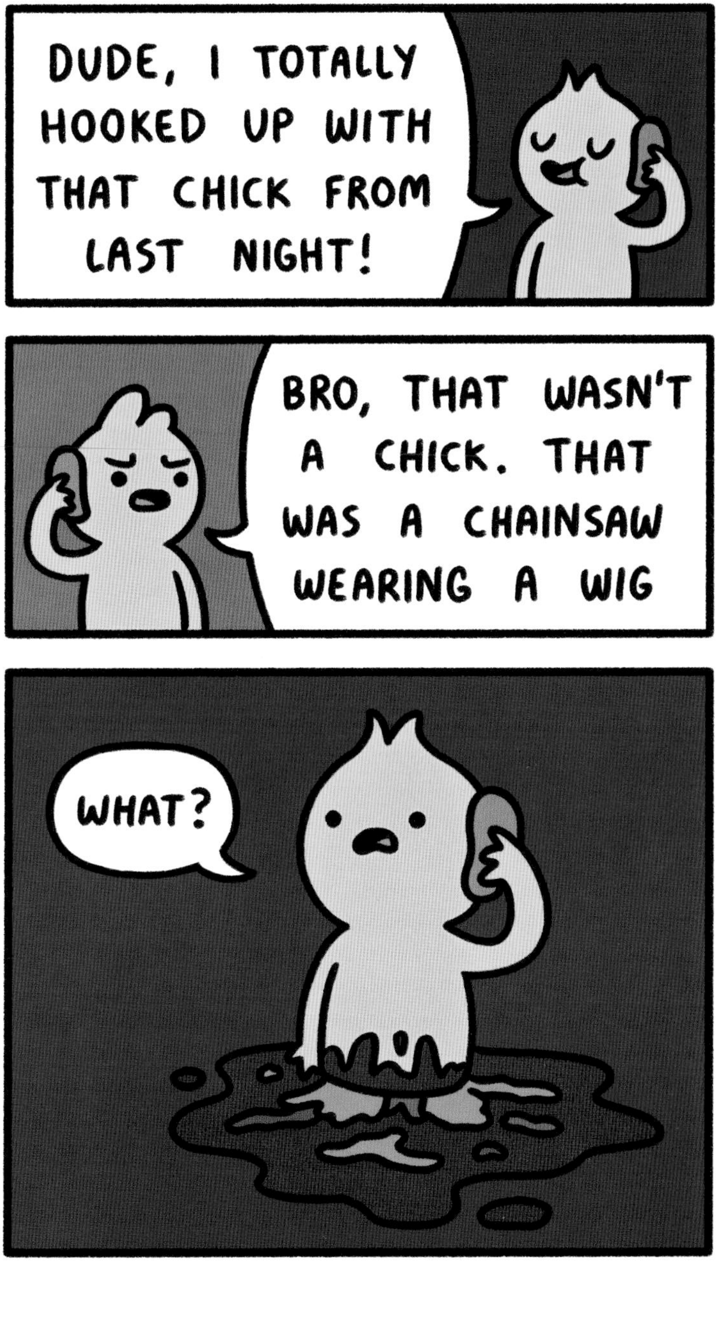
DUDE, I TOTALLY HOOKED UP WITH THAT CHICK FROM LAST NIGHT!
BRO, THAT WASN'T A CHICK. THAT WAS A CHAINSAW WEARING A WIG
WHAT?

OKAY JOKEBOT, MAKE ME LAUGH
WHAT'S EVERYONE'S LEAST FAVOURITE ETHNIC MINORITY?

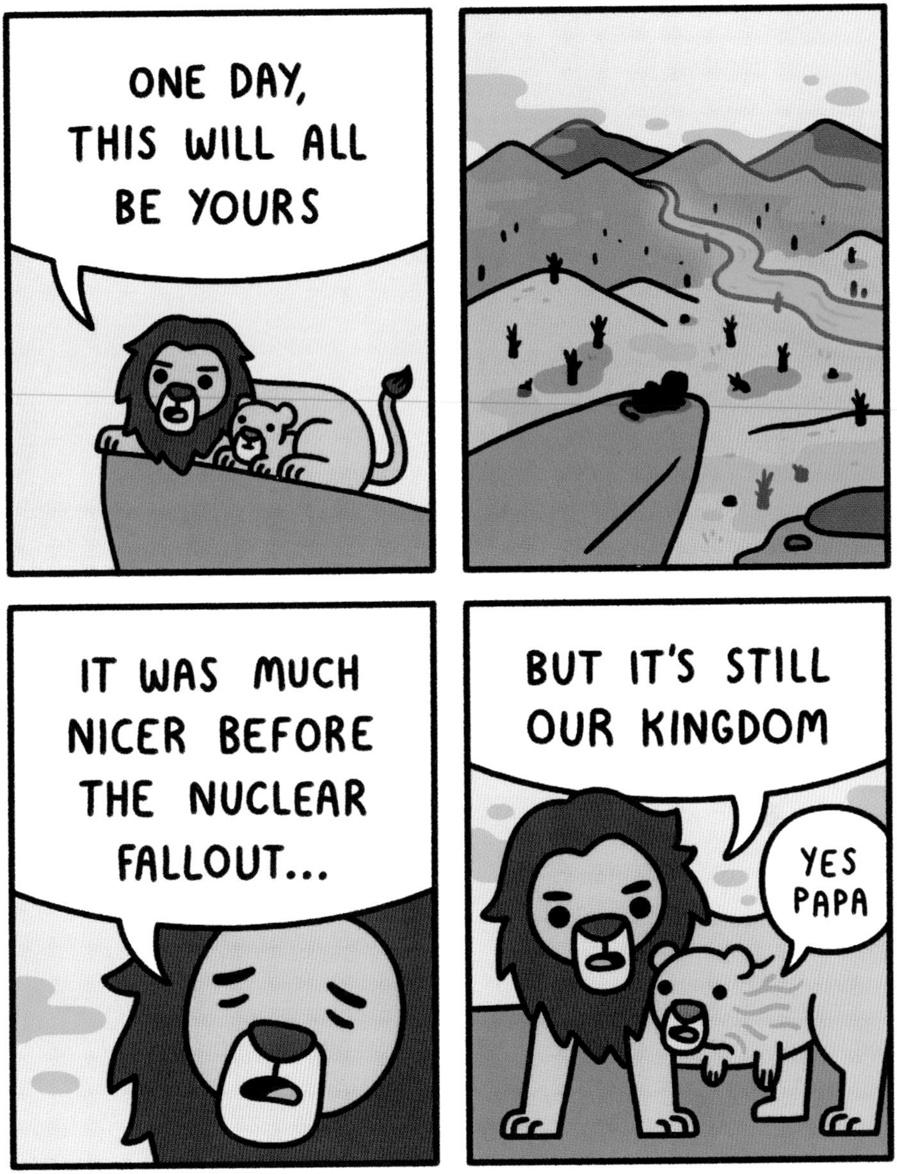
ONE DAY, THIS WILL ALL BE YOURS
IT WAS MUCH NICER BEFORE THE NUCLEAR FALLOUT...
BUT IT'S STILL OUR KINGDOM
YES PAPA

AND THE AWARD FOR 'BIGGEST STAR' GOES TO...
LEONARDO DICAPRIO
CLAP CLAP

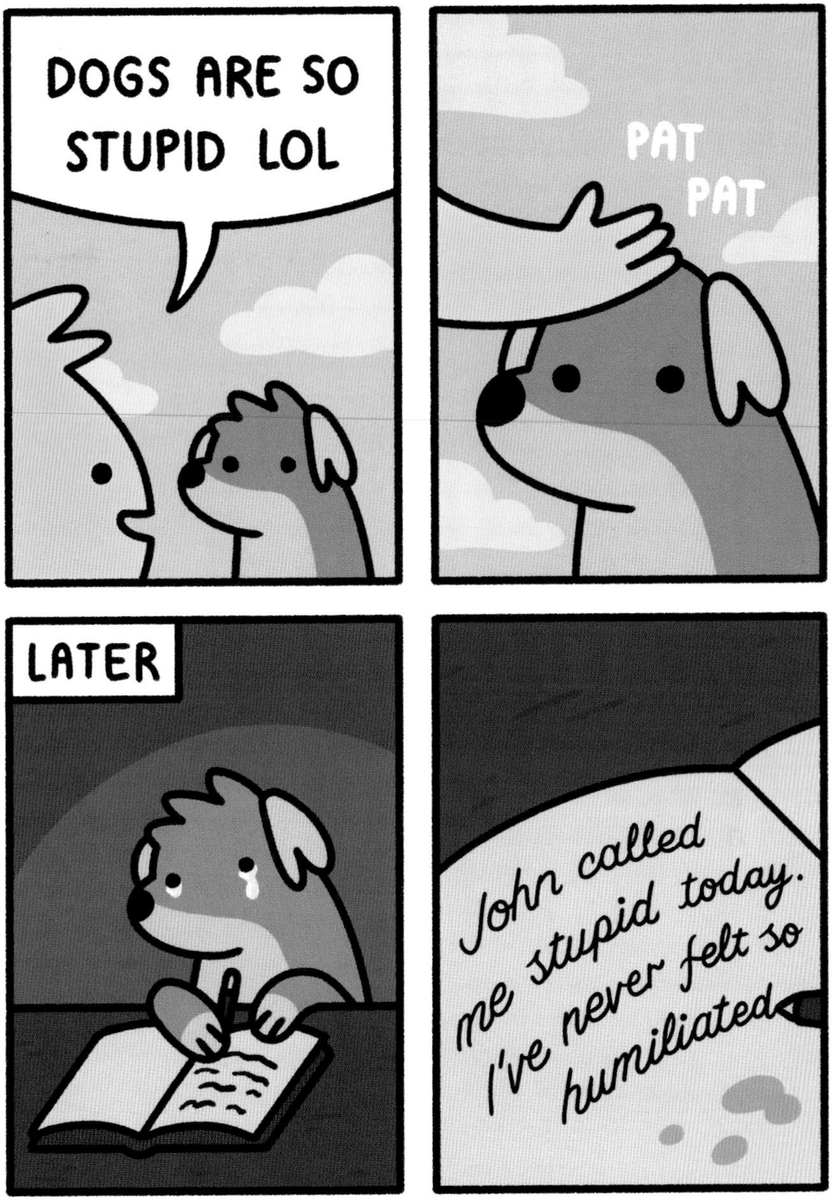
DOGS ARE SO STUPID LOL
PAT PAT
LATER
John called me stupid today. I've never felt so humiliated

YOU'VE GOT A NEW FOLLOWER!
TED
@TED1

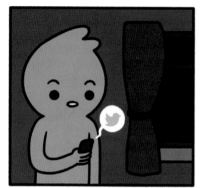

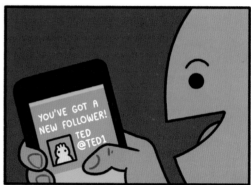

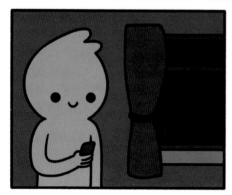

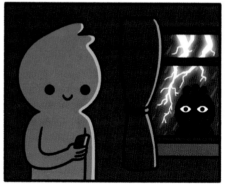

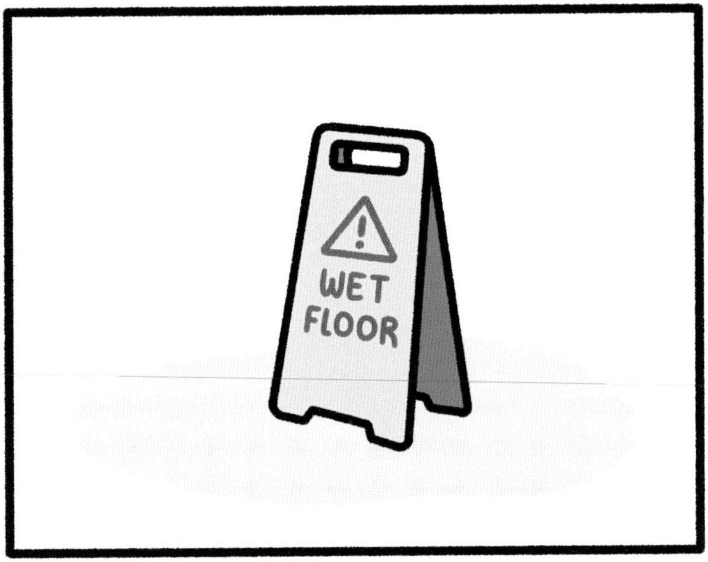
WET
FLOOR

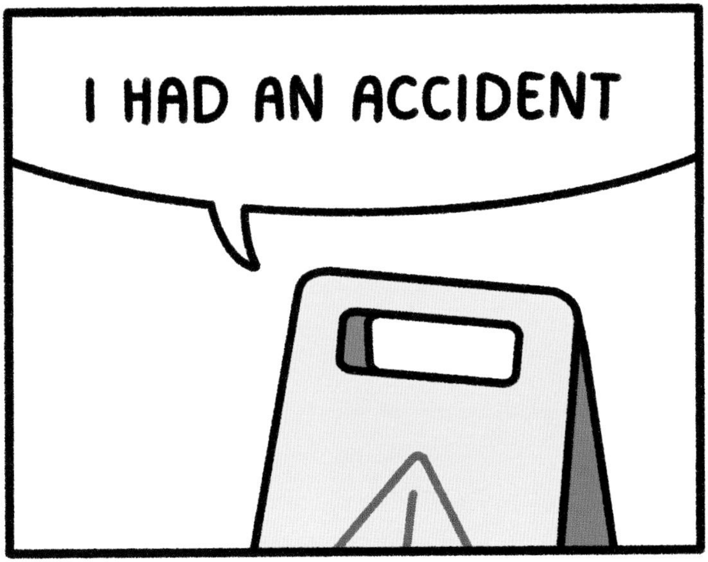
I HAD AN ACCIDENT

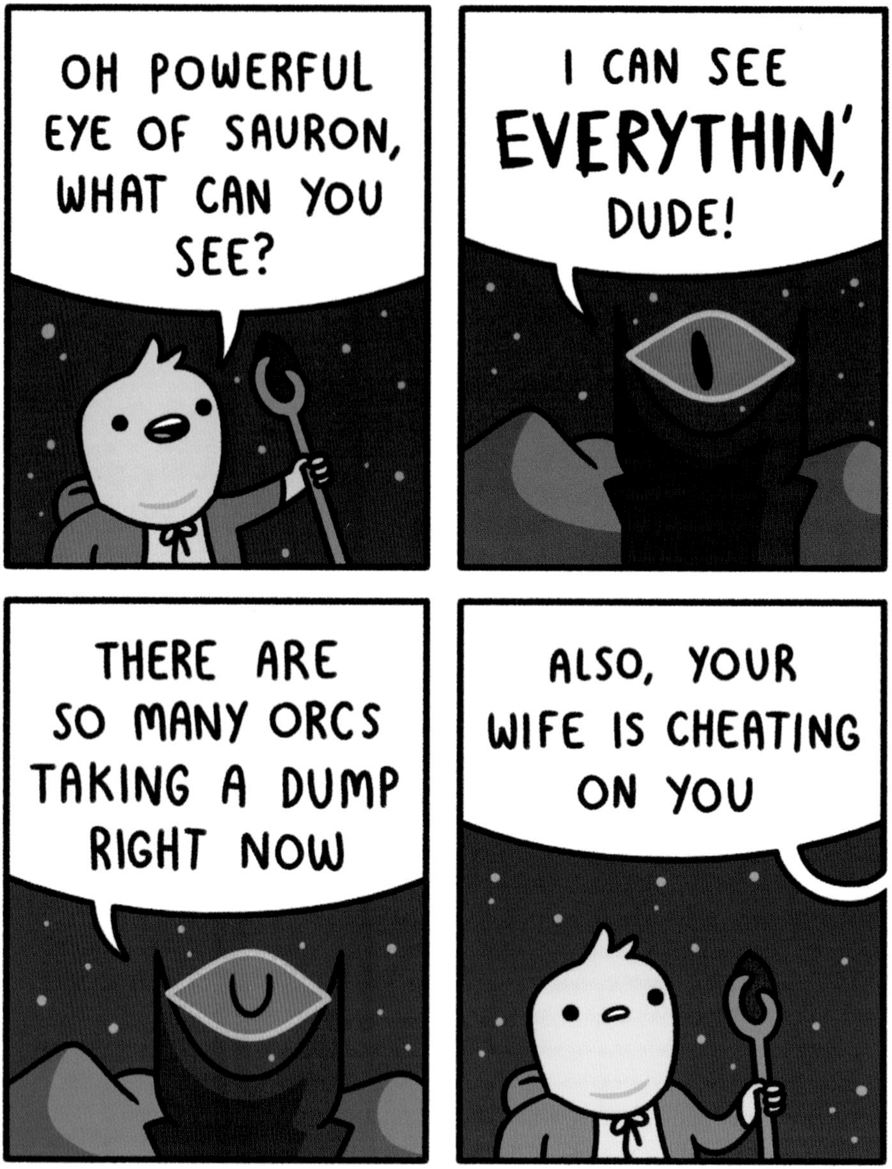
OH POWERFUL EYE OF SAURON, WHAT CAN YOU SEE?
I CAN SEE EVERYTHIN', DUDE!
THERE ARE SO MANY ORCS TAKING A DUMP RIGHT NOW
ALSO, YOUR WIFE IS CHEATING ON YOU

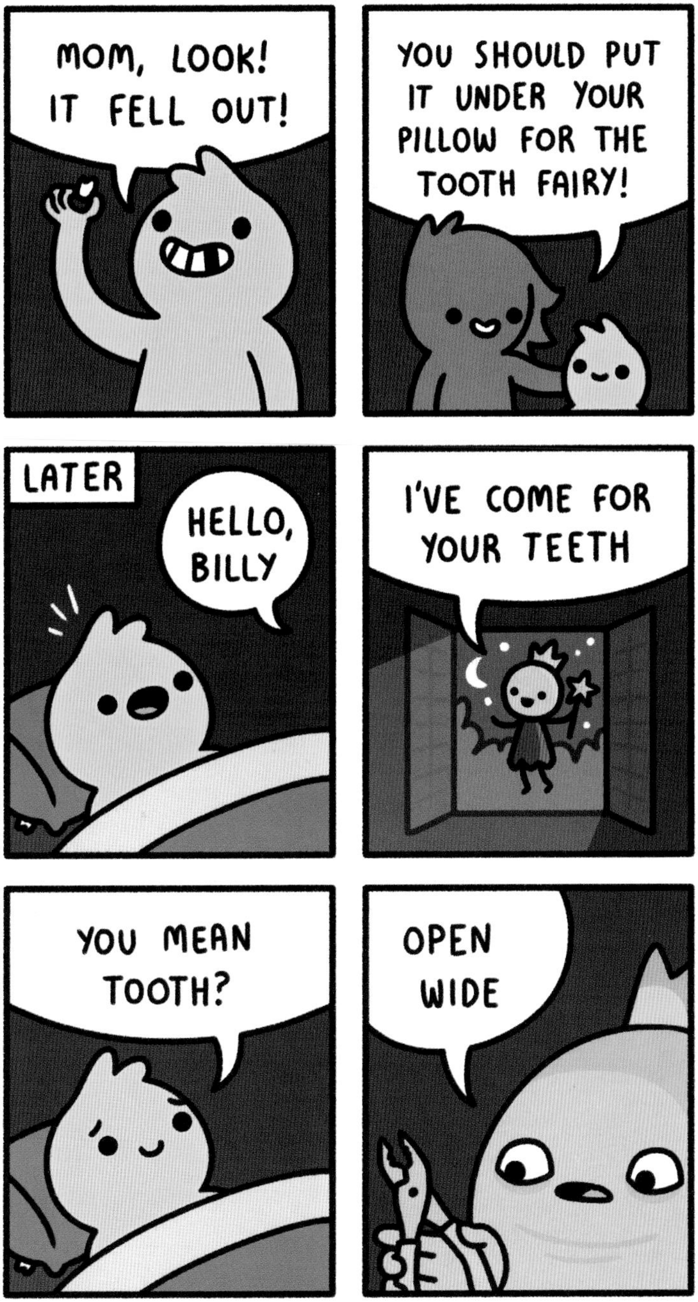
MOM, LOOK! IT FELL OUT!
YOU SHOULD PUT IT UNDER YOUR PILLOW FOR THE TOOTH FAIRY!
LATER
HELLO, BILLY
I'VE COME FOR YOUR TEETH
YOU MEAN TOOTH?
OPEN WIDE

BAD NEWS FOR THOSE WITH ALLERGIES
TODAY'S POLLEN COUNT WILL BE THE HIGHEST IN HISTORY
OH MY GOD
OH MY GOD!

SOME ANIMALS HAVE GREAT CAMOUFLAGE

ARCTIC FOX

DESERT VIPER

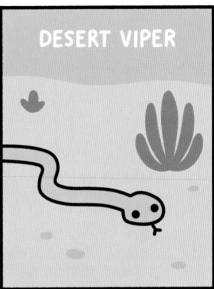

STICK INSECT

JERRY (AT A PARTY)

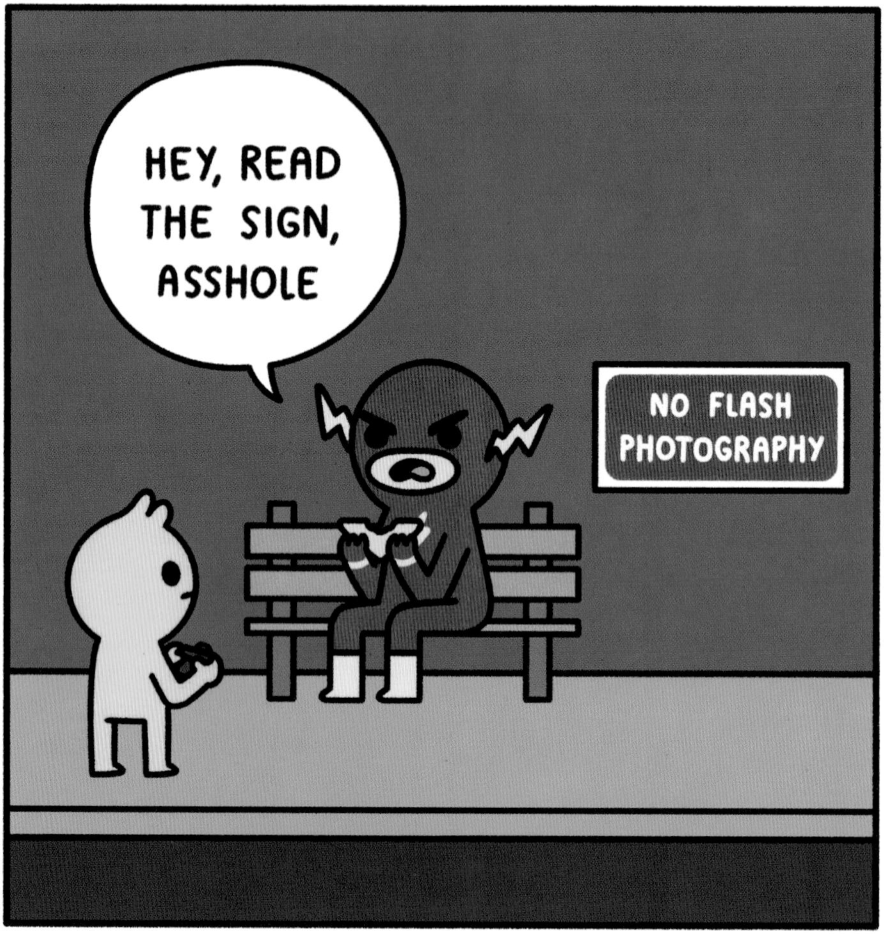
HEY, READ THE SIGN, ASSHOLE
NO FLASH PHOTOGRAPHY

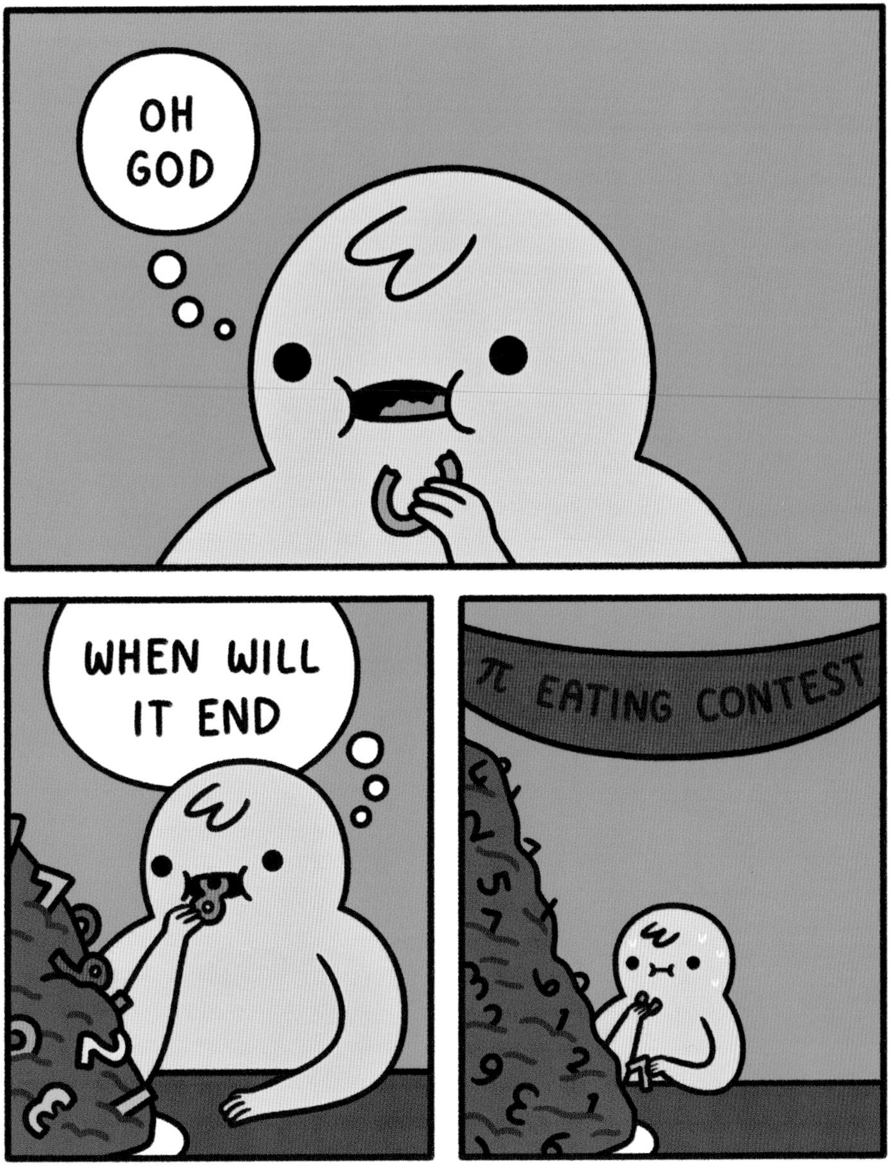
OH GOD
WHEN WILL IT END
π EATING CONTEST

BEING A SNAKE CHARMER REQUIRES NERVES OF STEEL
TO ME, YOU ARE PERFECT
OH MY!

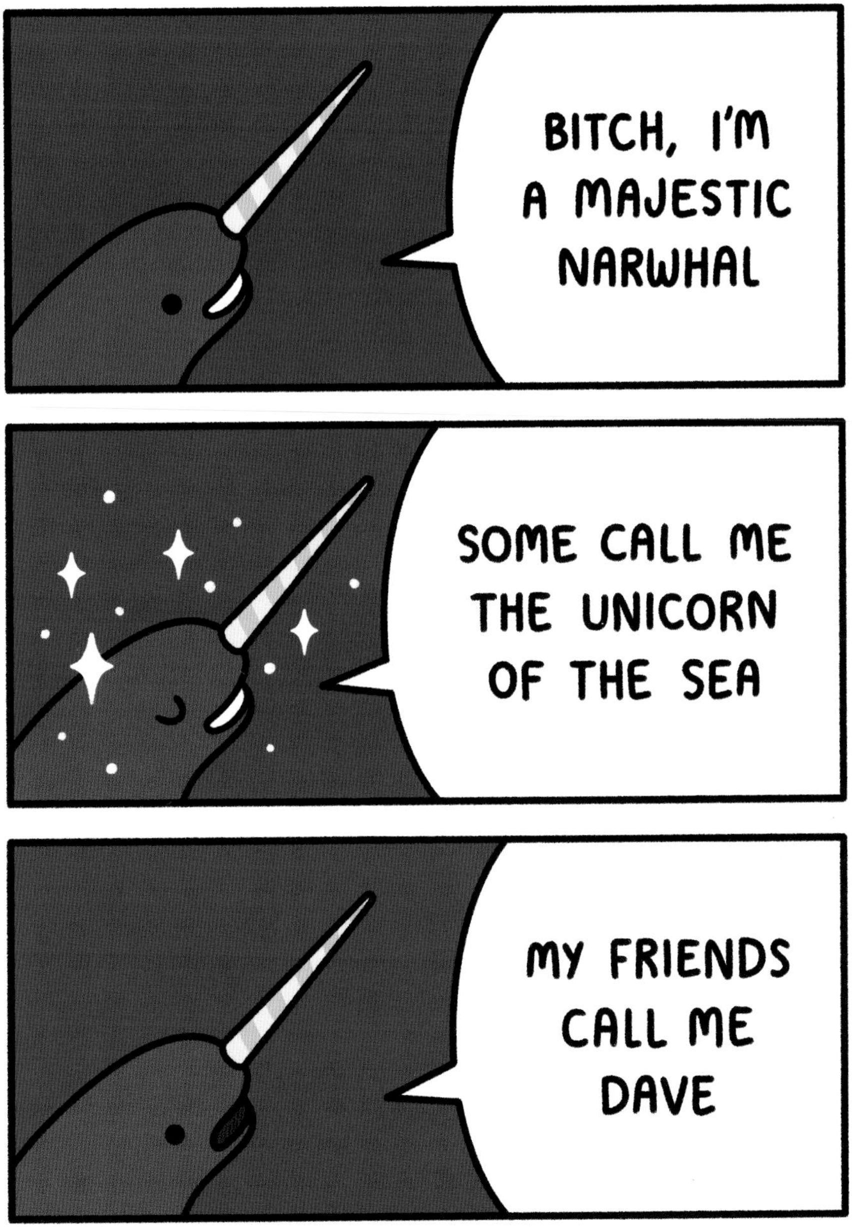
BITCH, I'M A MAJESTIC NARWHAL
SOME CALL ME THE UNICORN OF THE SEA
MY FRIENDS CALL ME DAVE

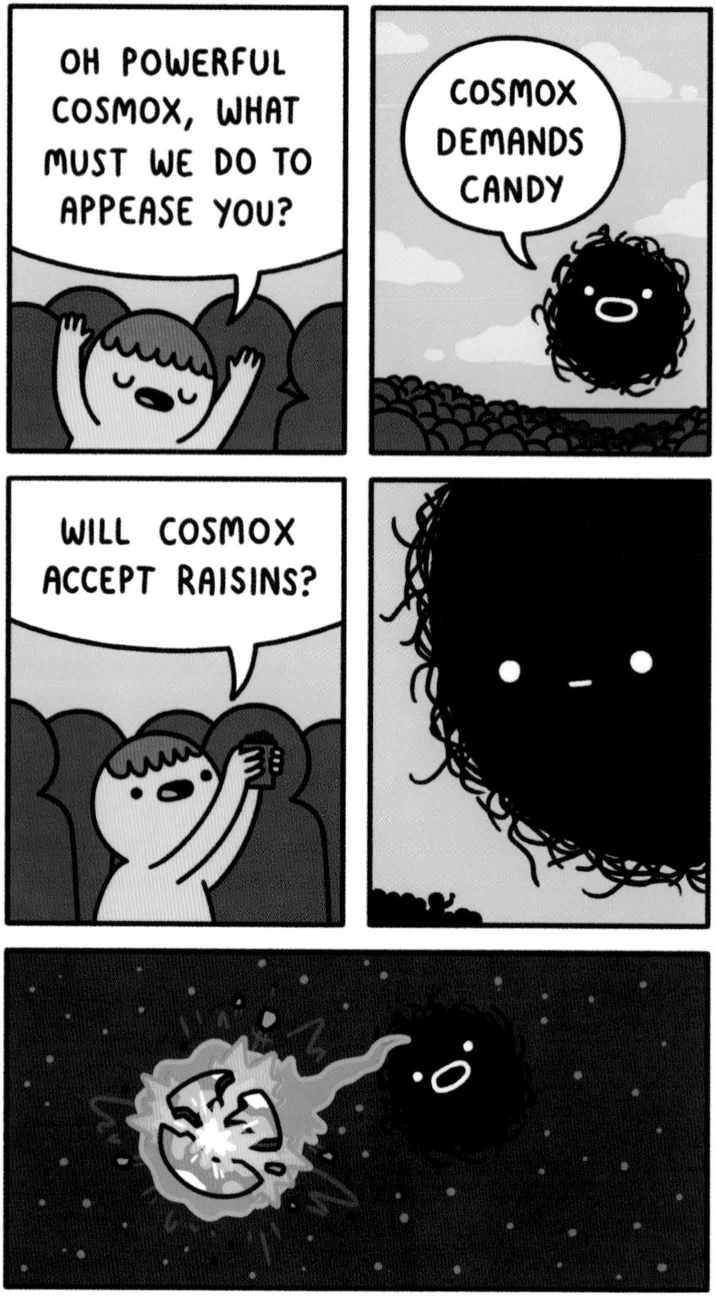
OH POWERFUL COSMOX, WHAT MUST WE DO TO APPEASE YOU?
COSMOX DEMANDS CANDY
WILL COSMOX ACCEPT RAISINS?

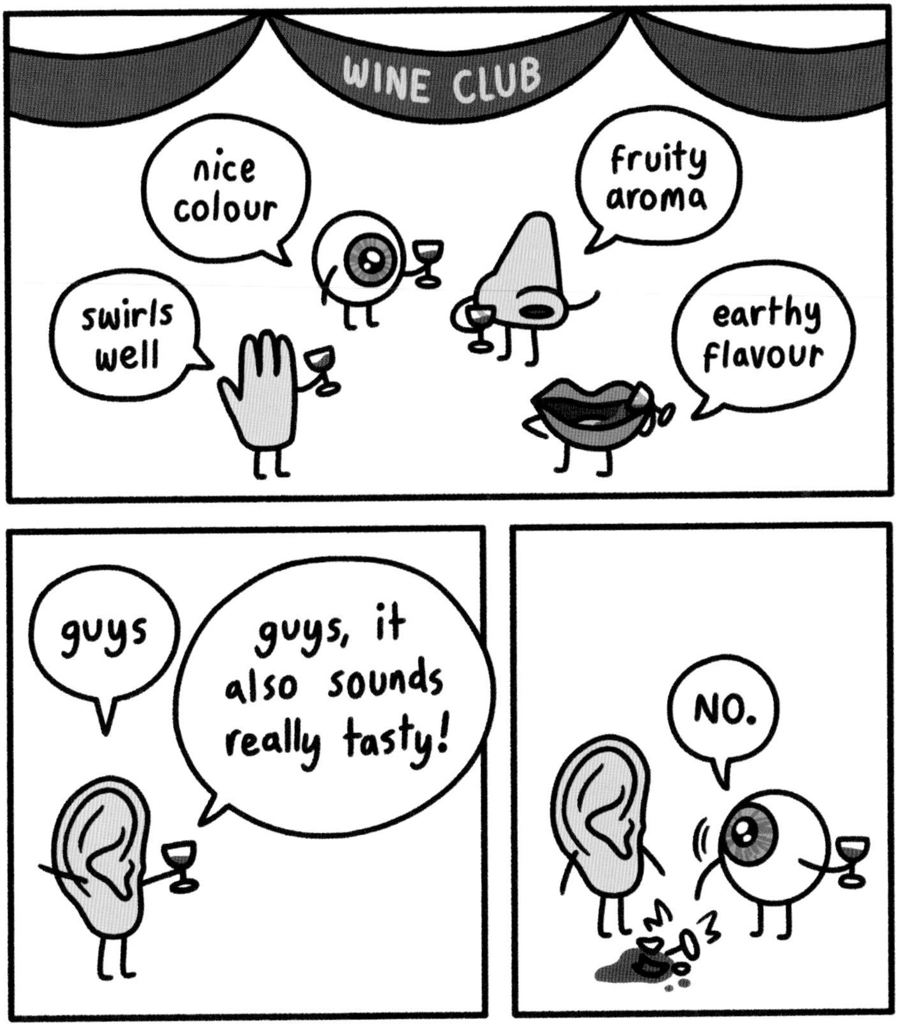
WINE CLUB
nice colour
fruity aroma
swirls well
earthy flavour
guys
guys, it also sounds really tasty!
NO.

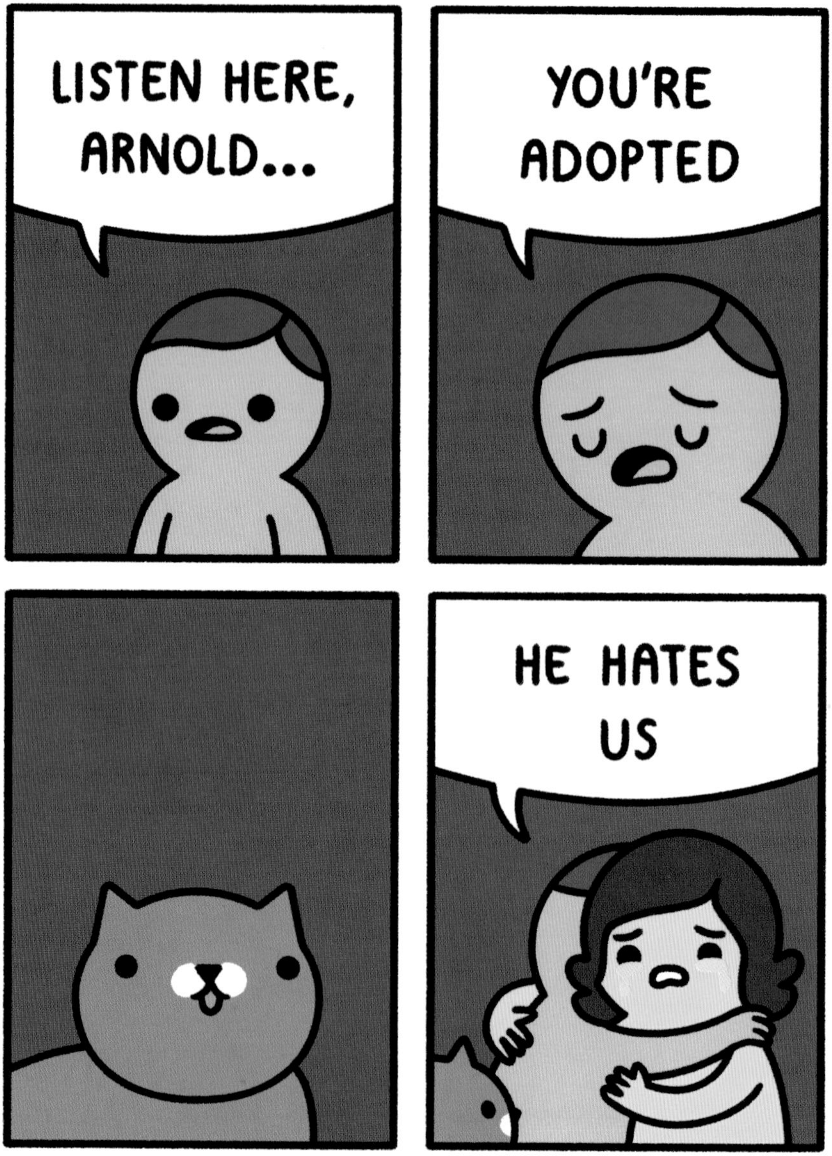
LISTEN HERE, ARNOLD...
YOU'RE ADOPTED
HE HATES US

BEAUTIFUL PIECE
WHAT WAS YOUR INSPIRATION?
YOUR MOTHER

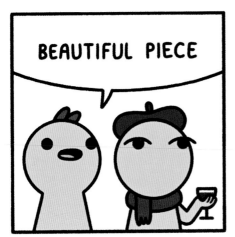

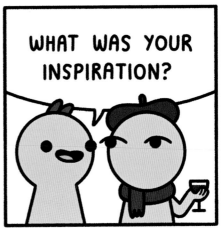

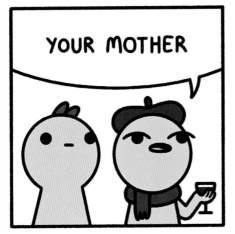

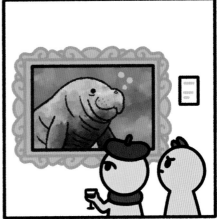

KARAOKE
KARAOKE
KARAOKE
WHY DOES HE ALWAYS PICK BEETHOVEN?

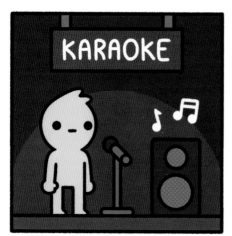

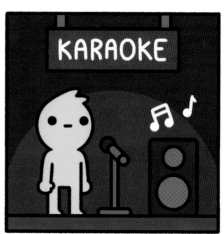

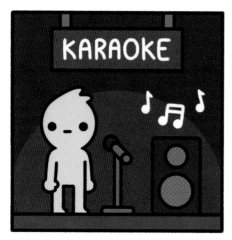

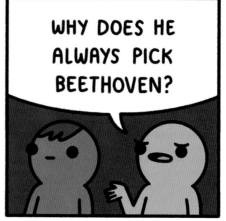

son, it's time we had the sex talk
do it
do it as much as possible
life is short

HOW 2 NINJA
WHY ARE YOU READING THAT NONSENSE?
SHUT UP JANICE, THIS DOESN'T INVOLVE YOU
LATER
JANICE, HELP

I LOVE YOU, MUM
OH GOD, OH GOD
I'M A MONSTER

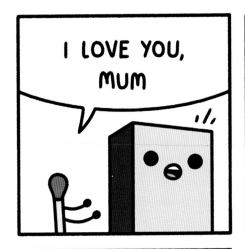

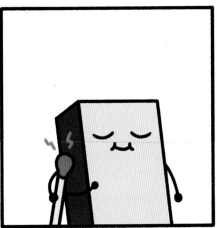

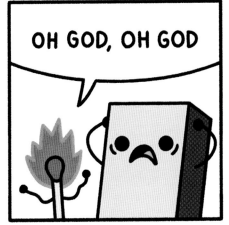

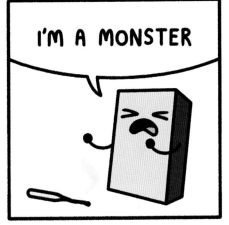

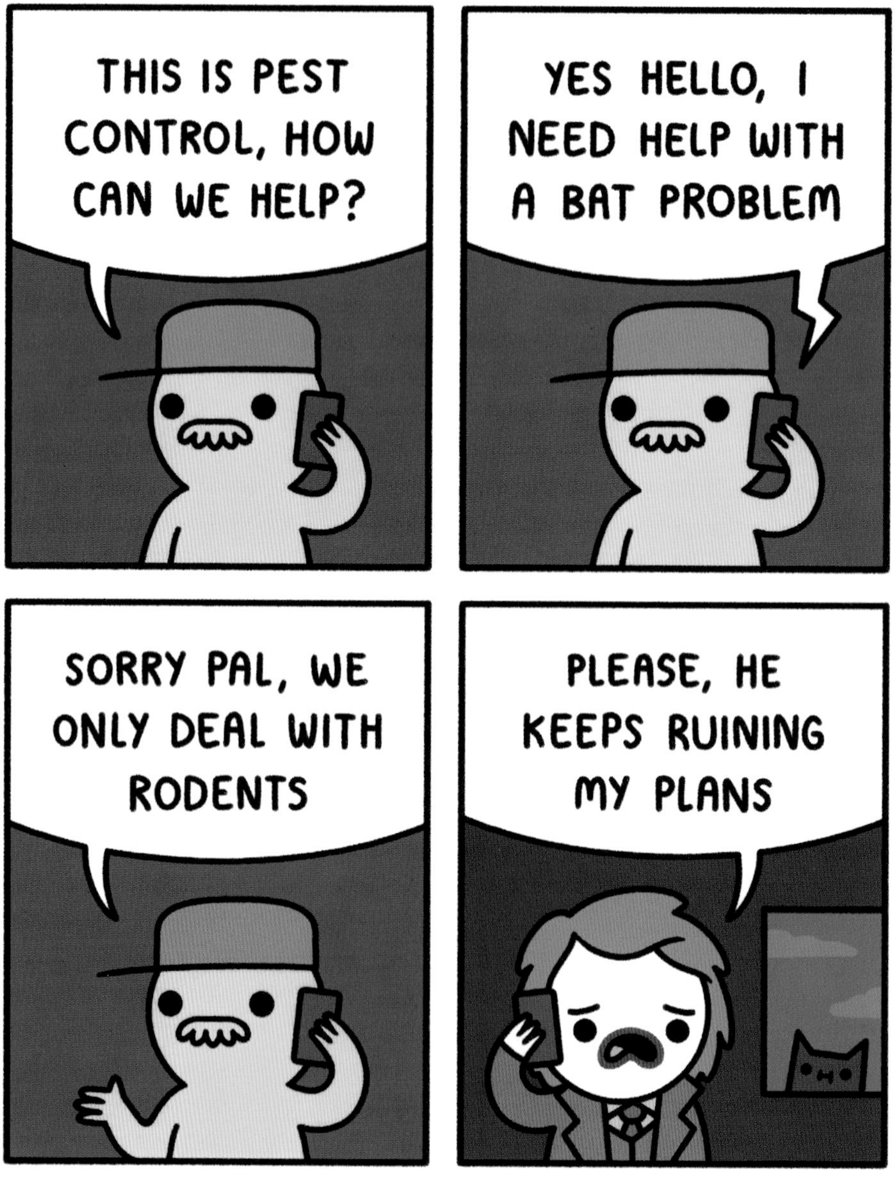
THIS IS PEST CONTROL, HOW CAN WE HELP?
YES HELLO, I NEED HELP WITH A BAT PROBLEM
SORRY PAL, WE ONLY DEAL WITH RODENTS
PLEASE, HE KEEPS RUINING MY PLANS

THERE AIN'T NO MOUNTAIN HIGH ENOUGH...

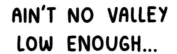
AIN'T NO VALLEY LOW ENOUGH...

AIN'T NO RIVER WIDE ENOUGH...

DON'T BE SO HARD ON YOURSELF. I THINK IT LOOKS GREAT

HEY
GIVE US A KISS
WILL IT TURN YOU INTO A PRINCE?
NO, I'M JUST REALLY HORNY

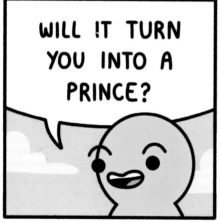

WHO'S A GOOD BOY?
ME! ME!
OKAY, THEN HELP ME BURY THIS BODY

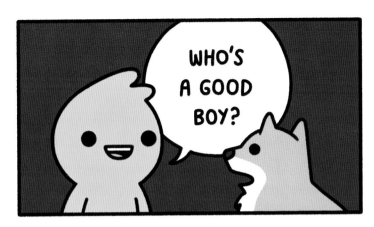

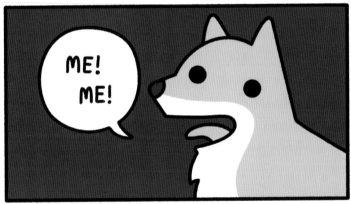

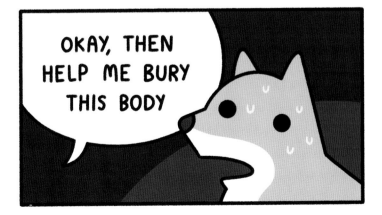

HEY, IT'S-A THE MARIO BROS!
MAMA, WHY-A YOU NEVER REMEMBER MY NAME?
I'M-A SORRY, GREEN MARIO

PLAYER 2
HAS JOINED

LET'S DO THIS

WHAT CAN I GET YOU?
I'LL HAVE THE STEAK, LOBSTER AND TWO SIDES OF FRIES
OH, ARE YOU EXPECTING COMPANY?
LADY, FOOD IS MY COMPANION

MUM, THERE'S A MONSTER UNDER MY BED!
IT'S THE MOST HIDEOUS THING I'VE EVER SEEN
WHY DO YOU HATE ME, BROTHER

GET AWAY RAT, YOU CARRIER OF DISEASE
I ALSO CARRY PRESENTS
AWW
IT'S ANTHRAX
GOD DAMMIT

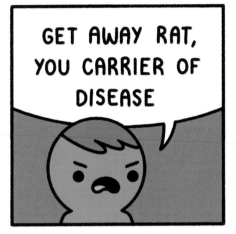

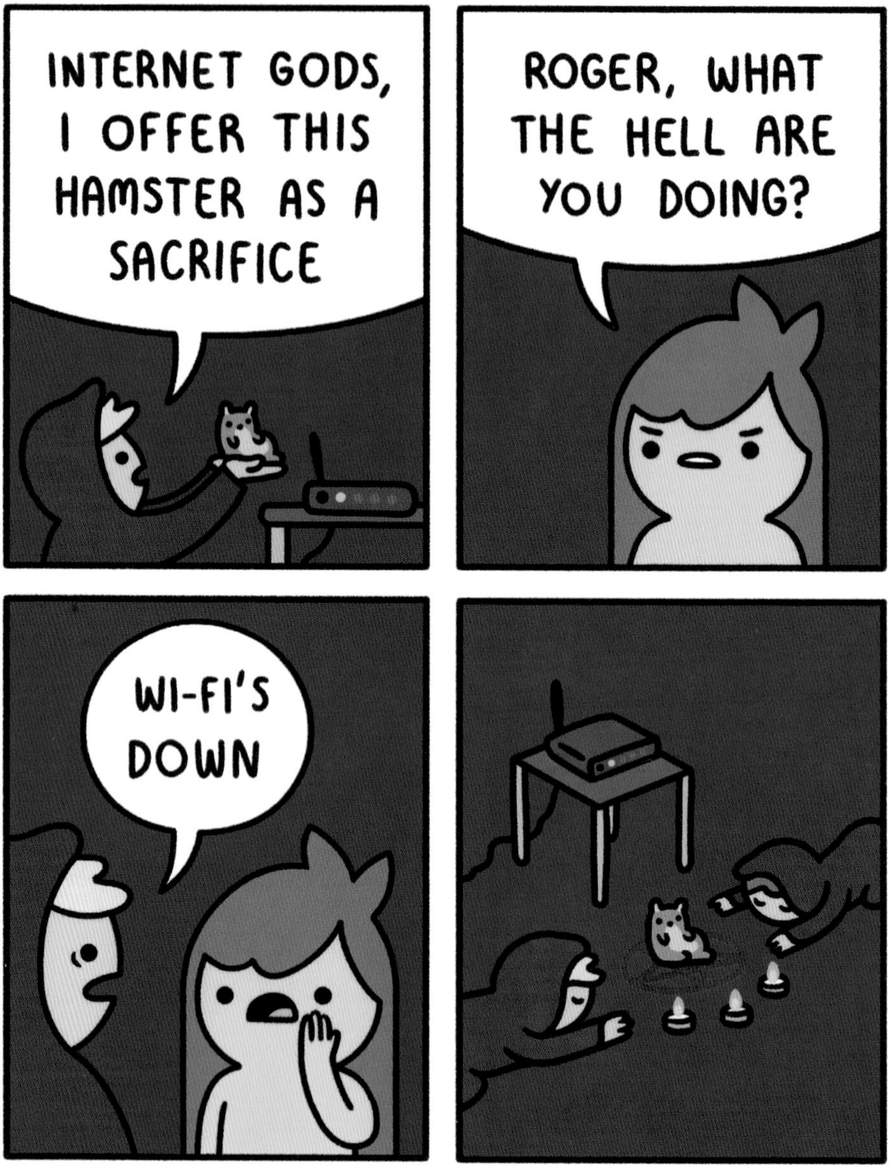
INTERNET GODS, I OFFER THIS HAMSTER AS A SACRIFICE
ROGER, WHAT THE HELL ARE YOU DOING?
WI-FI'S DOWN

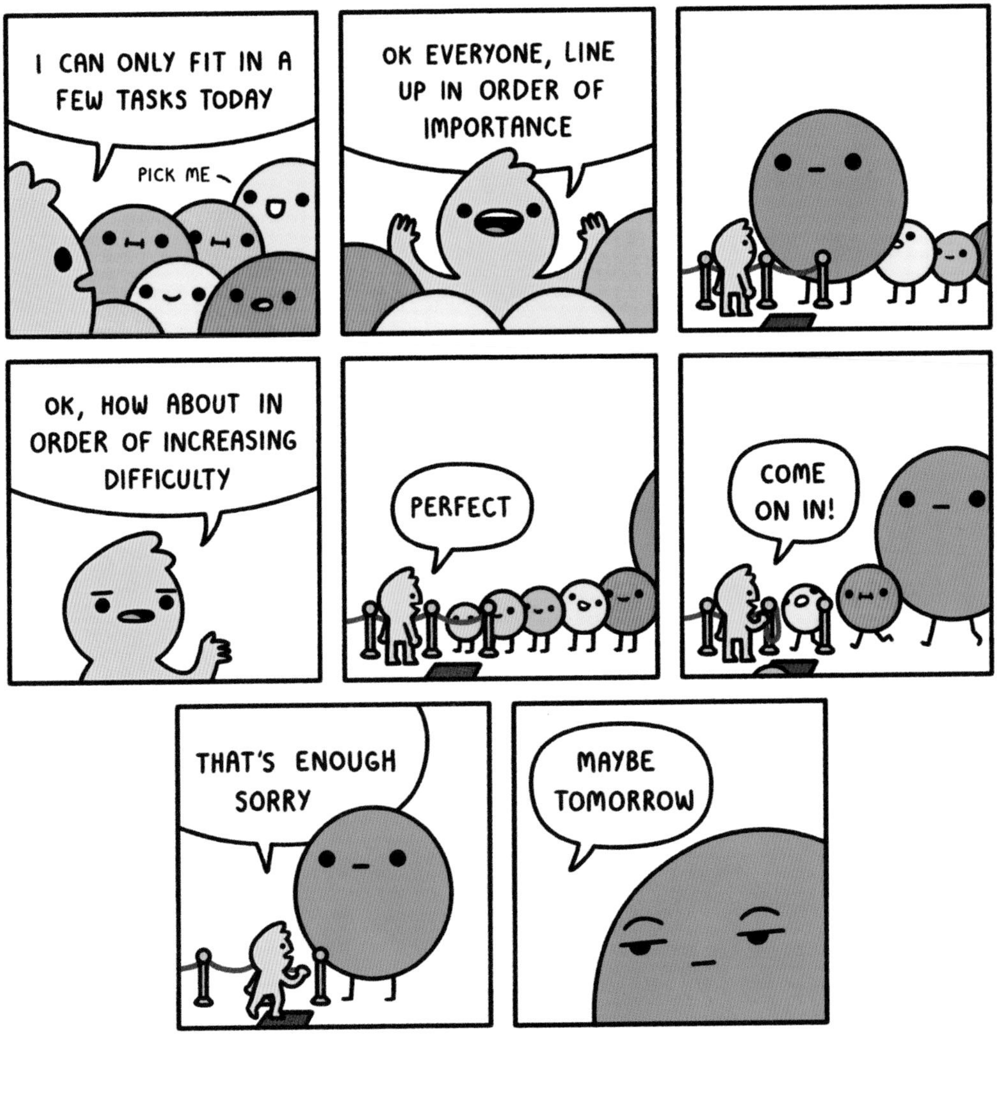
I CAN ONLY FIT IN A FEW TASKS TODAY
PICK ME
OK EVERYONE, LINE UP IN ORDER OF IMPORTANCE
OK, HOW ABOUT IN ORDER OF INCREASING DIFFICULTY
PERFECT
COME ON IN!
THAT'S ENOUGH SORRY
MAYBE TOMORROW

PASSPORT CONTROL
NEXT
I THINK THIS GUY'S A TERRORIST
NO, IT'S JUST AN OLD PICTURE, I SWEAR

GO PIKACHU!
GO GRANDMA!
CALL THE POLICE

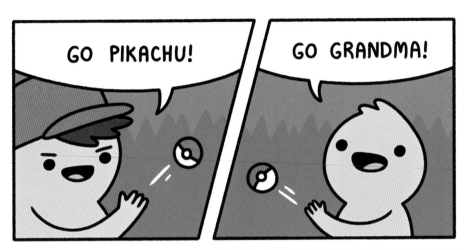

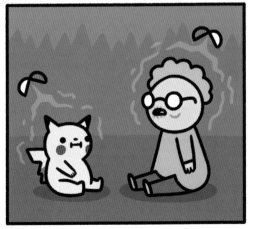

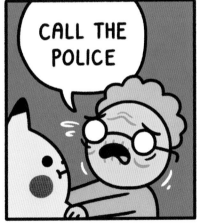

FREE HUGS
NO WAY, I'M NOT FALLING FOR THAT AGAIN
LAST TIME

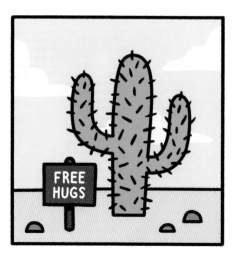

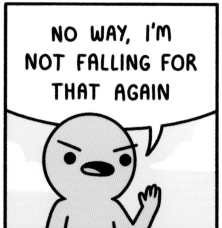

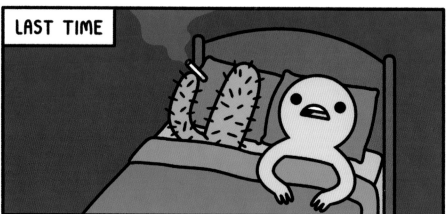

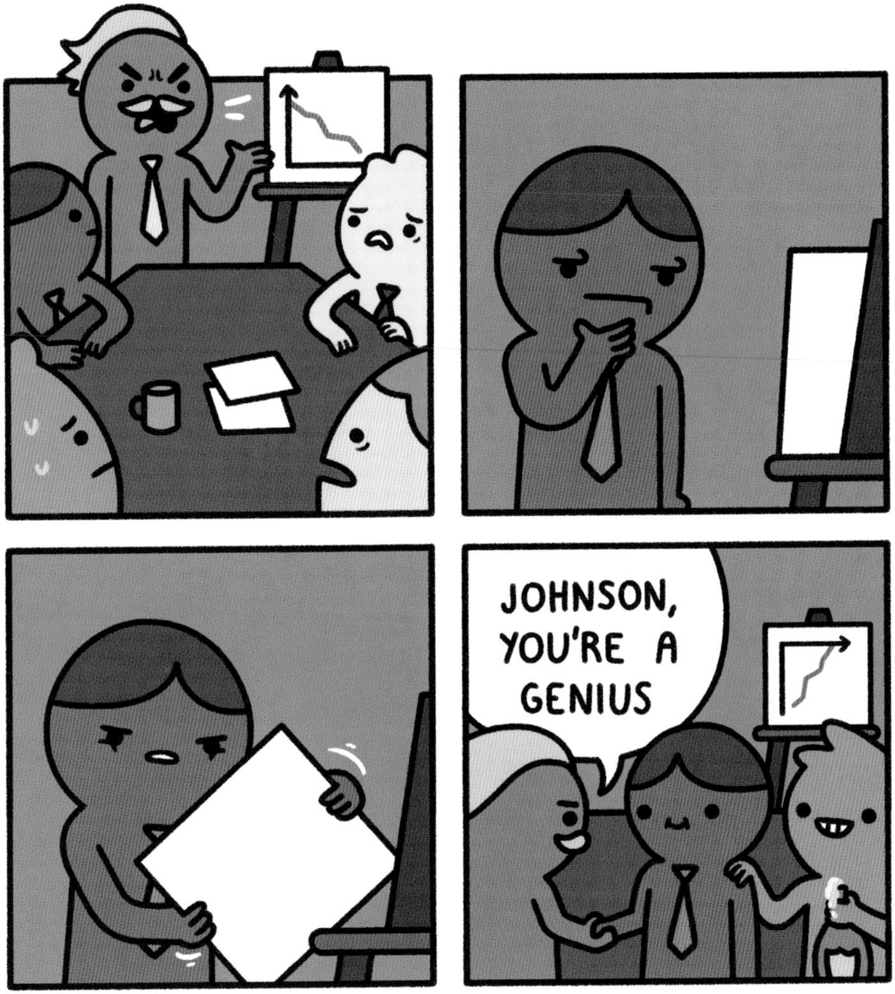
JOHNSON, YOU'RE A GENIUS

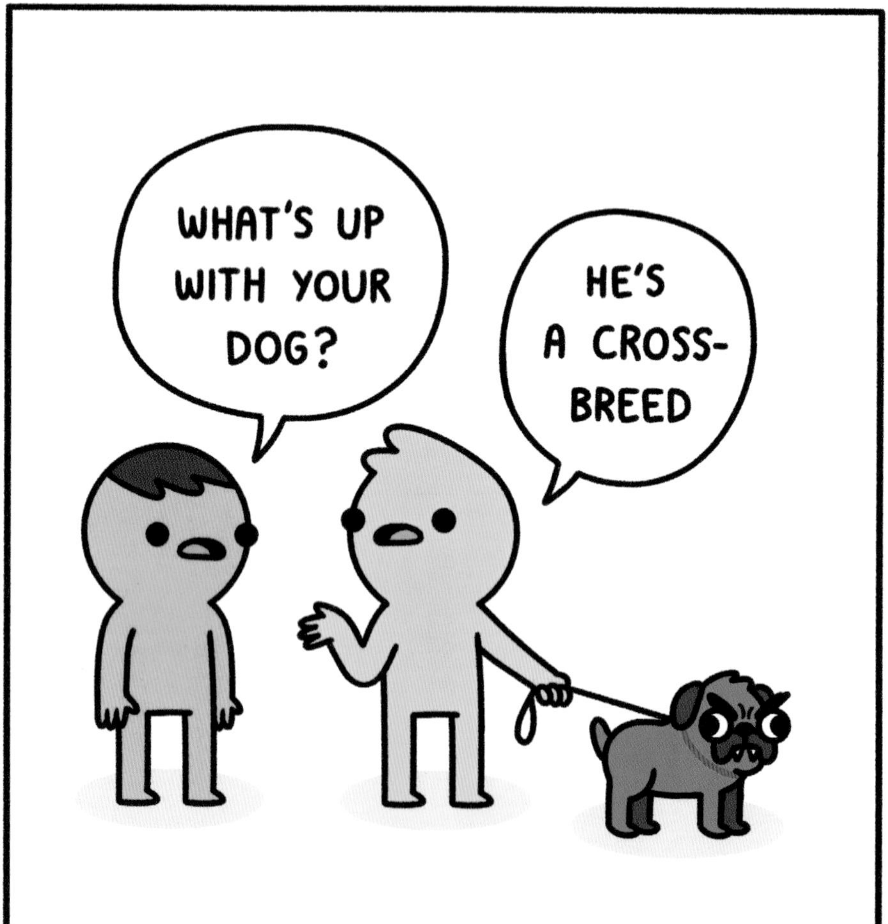
WHAT'S UP WITH YOUR DOG?
HE'S A CROSS-BREED

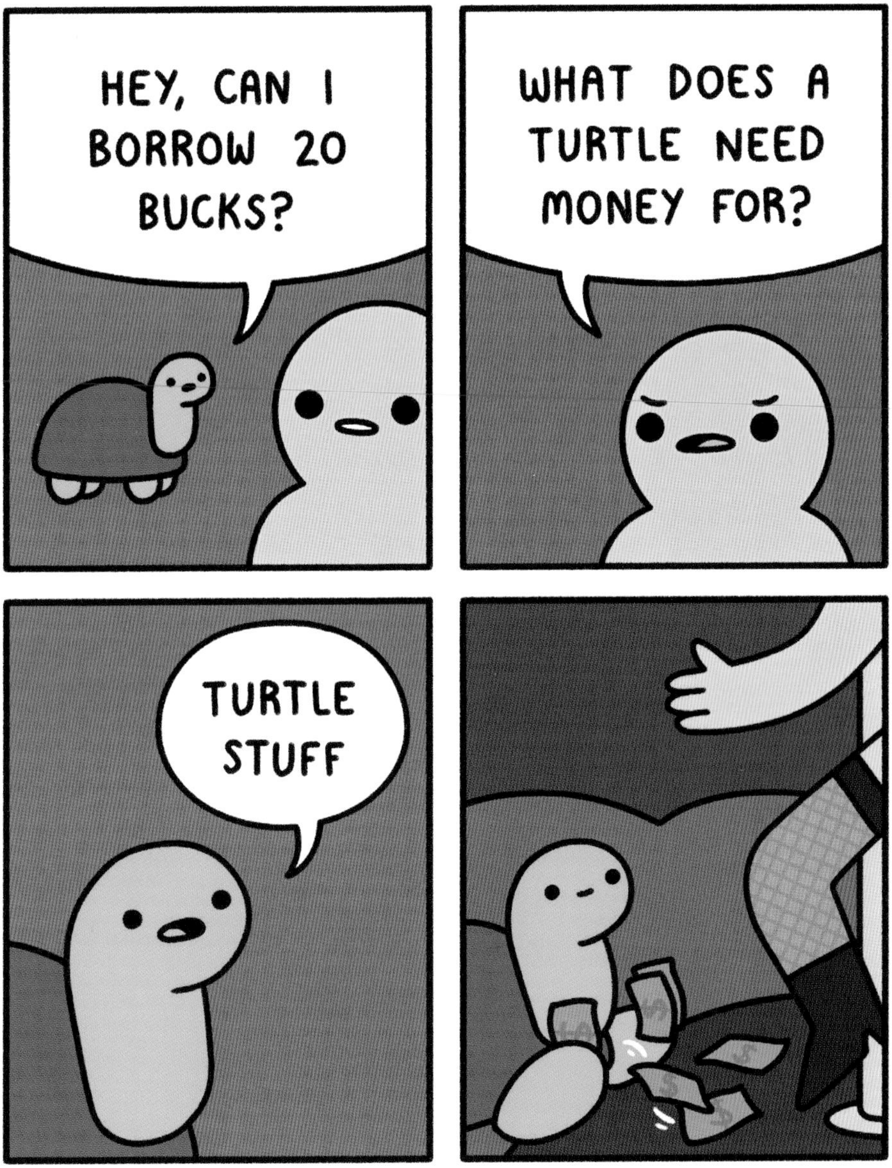
HEY, CAN I BORROW 20 BUCKS?
WHAT DOES A TURTLE NEED MONEY FOR?
TURTLE STUFF

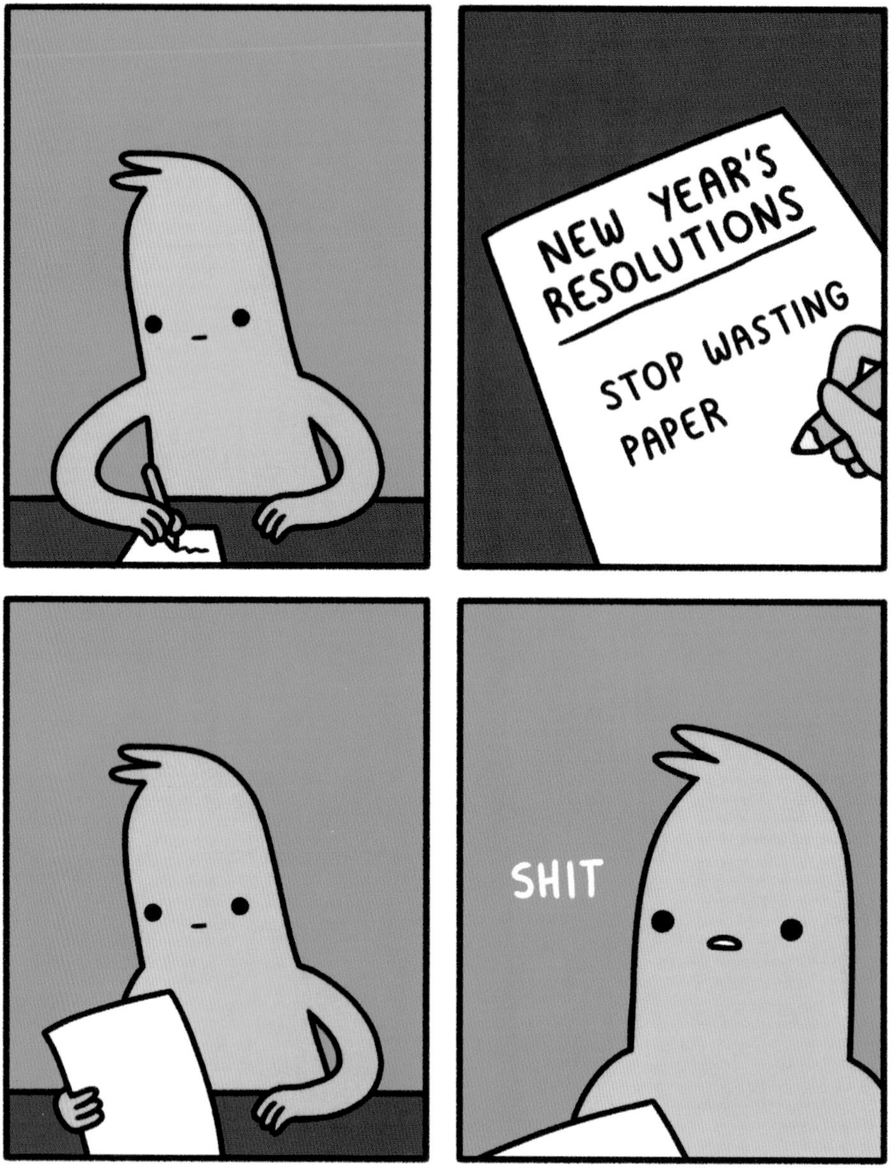
NEW YEAR'S RESOLUTIONS
STOP WASTING PAPER
SHIT

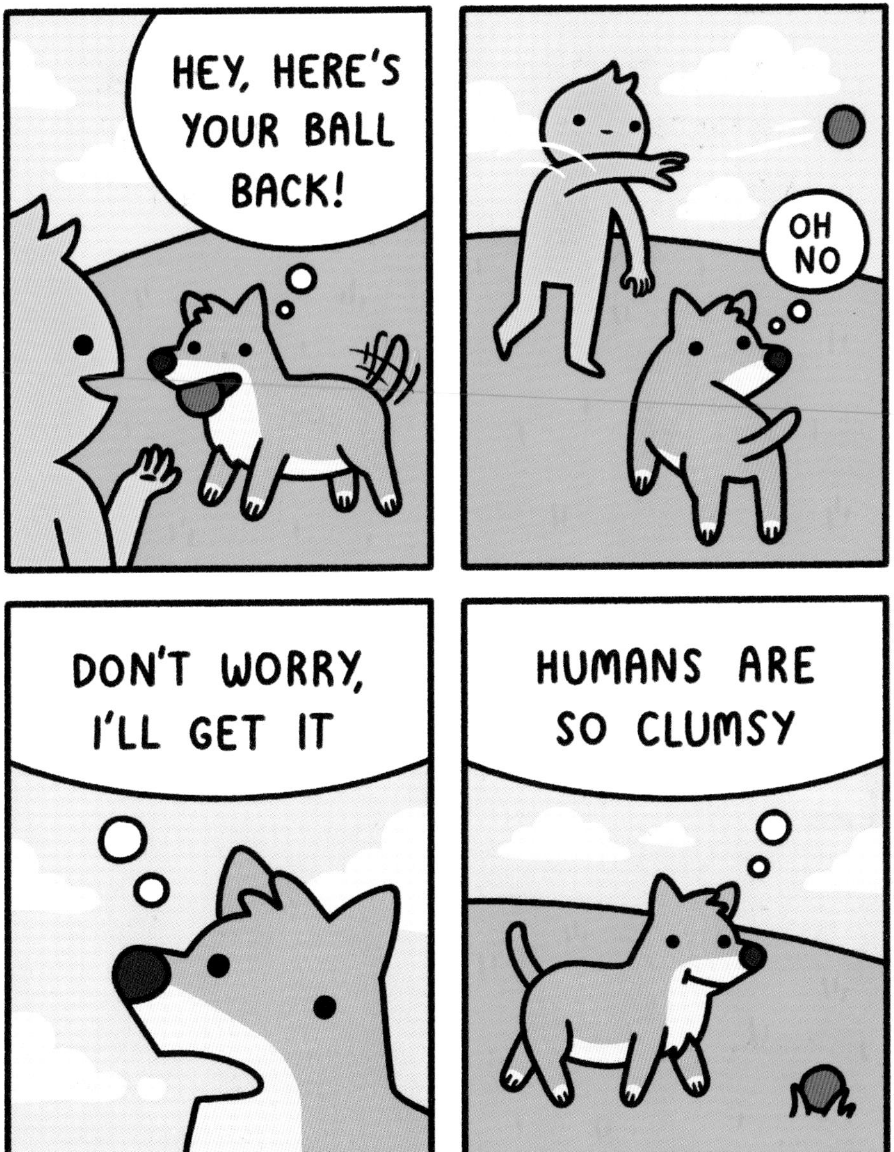
HEY, HERE'S YOUR BALL BACK!
OH NO
DON'T WORRY, I'LL GET IT
HUMANS ARE SO CLUMSY

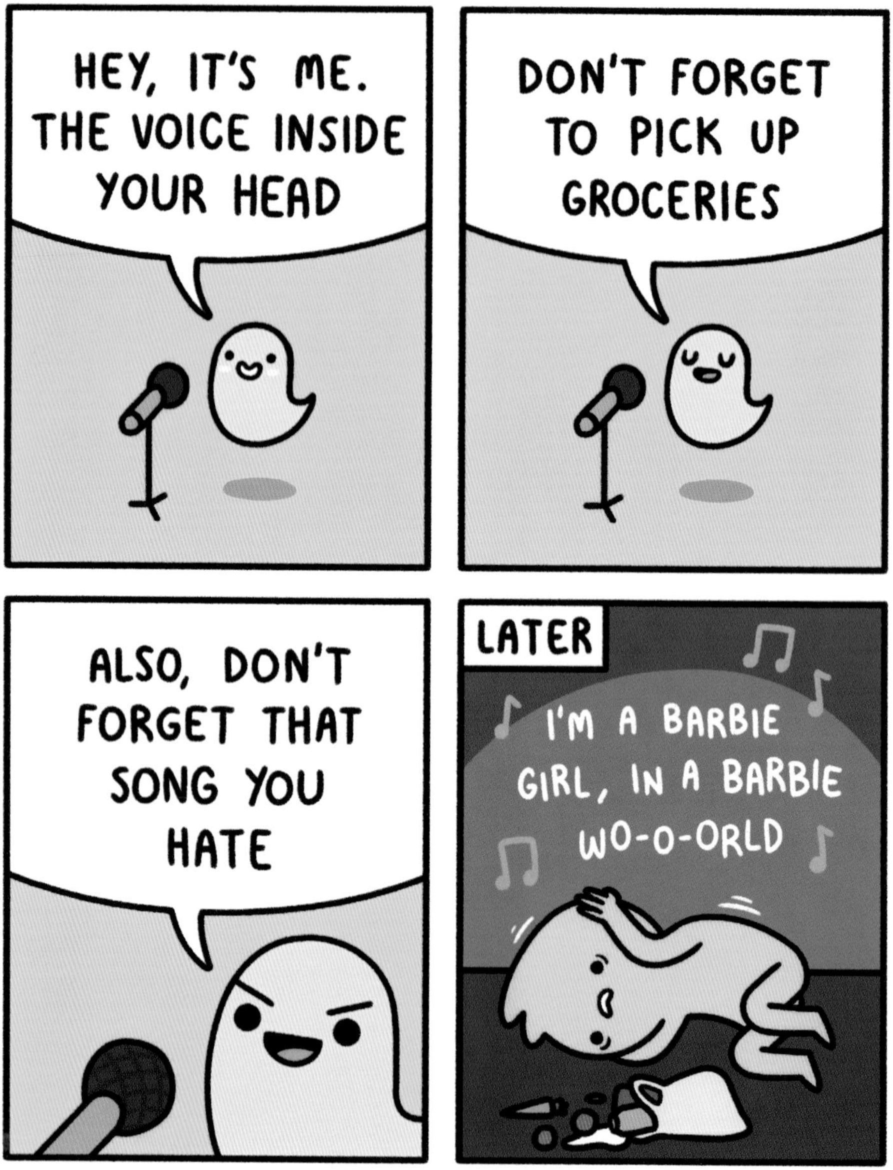
HEY, IT'S ME. THE VOICE INSIDE YOUR HEAD
DON'T FORGET TO PICK UP GROCERIES
ALSO, DON'T FORGET THAT SONG YOU HATE
LATER
I'M A BARBIE GIRL, IN A BARBIE WO-O-ORLD

RUDOLPH, HOW DO REINDEER FLY?
OUR SECRET IS MAGICAL CHRISTMAS DUST!

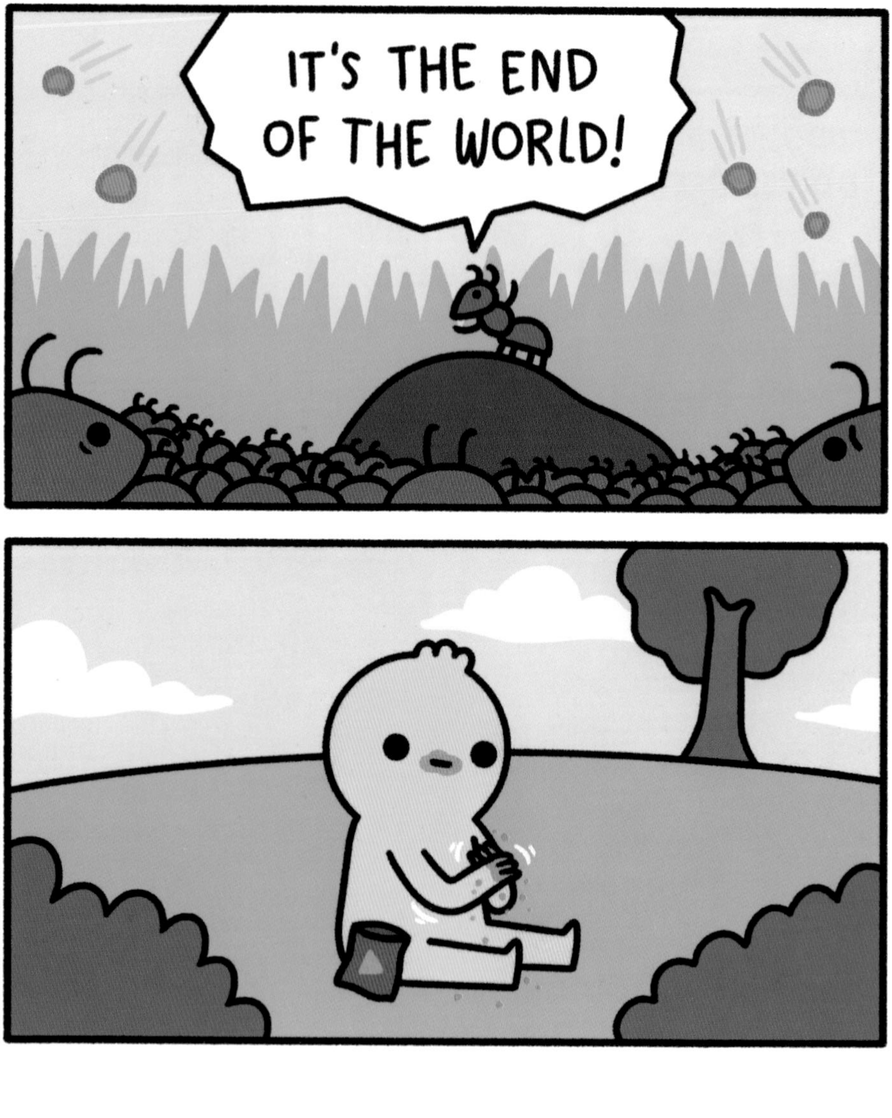
IT'S THE END OF THE WORLD!

do you know how fast you were going back there?
sorry officer, i'm desperate for a poo
clear a path
we got a code brown

MOVIE TRAILER EXPECTATION:

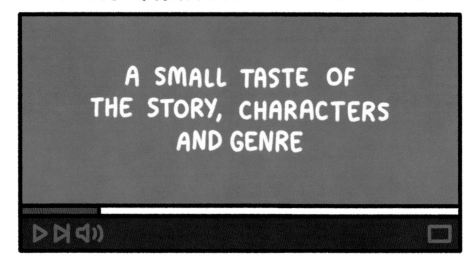

A SMALL TASTE OF
THE STORY, CHARACTERS
AND GENRE

MOVIE TRAILER REALITY:

THE ENTIRE PLOT
SUMMARIZED IN TWO MINUTES
BECAUSE FUCK YOU

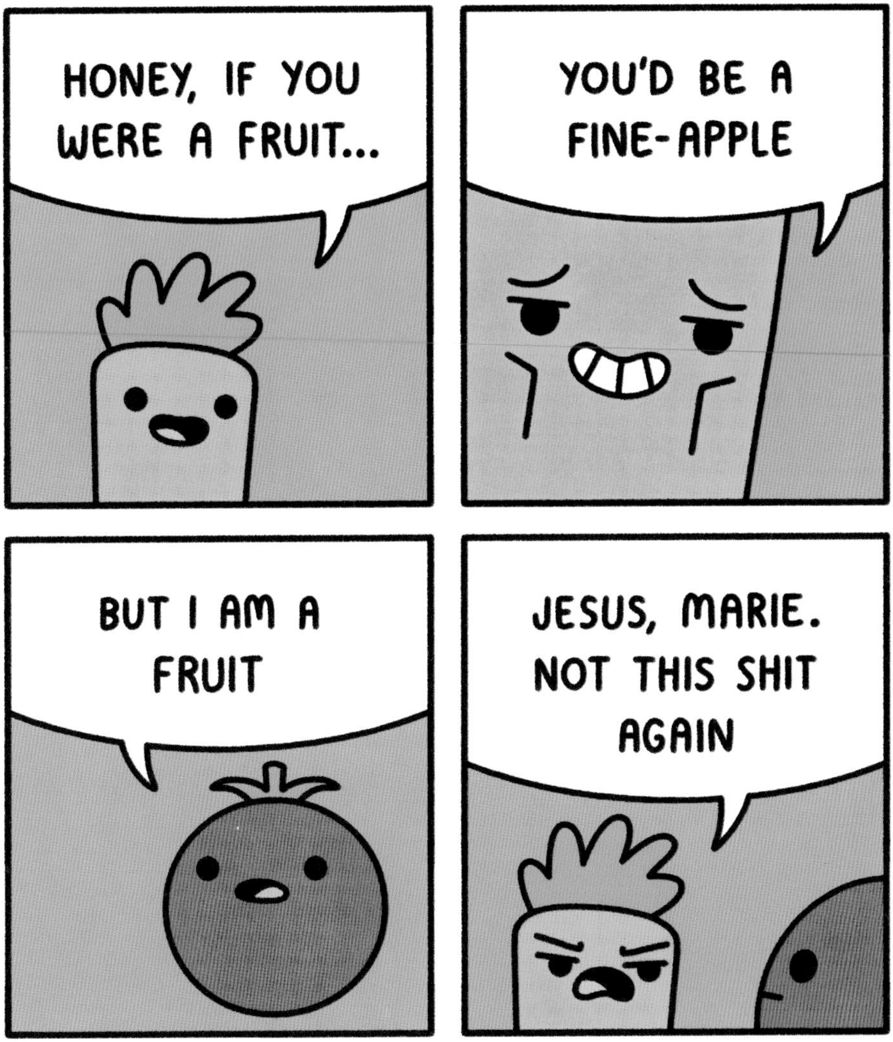
HONEY, IF YOU WERE A FRUIT...
YOU'D BE A FINE-APPLE
BUT I AM A FRUIT
JESUS, MARIE. NOT THIS SHIT AGAIN

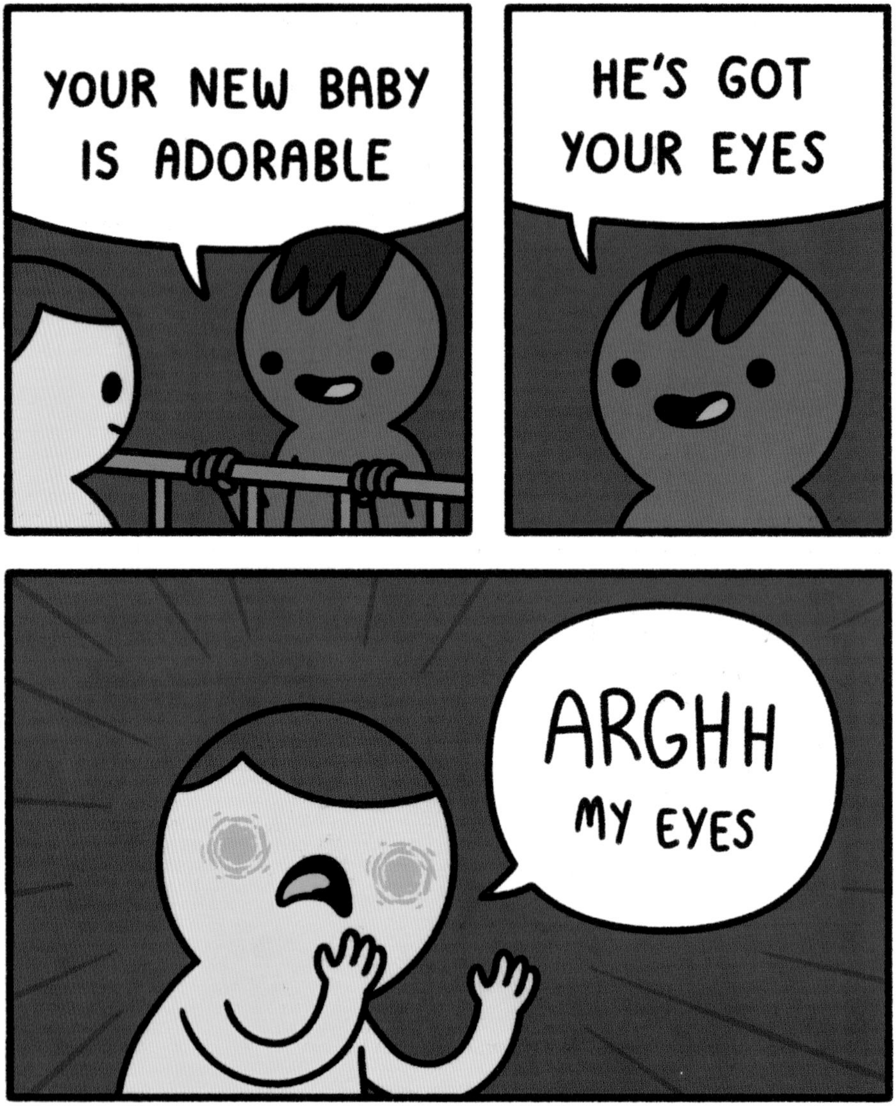
YOUR NEW BABY IS ADORABLE
HE'S GOT YOUR EYES
ARGHH
MY EYES

what's the deal with werewolves?
you suck
thank you

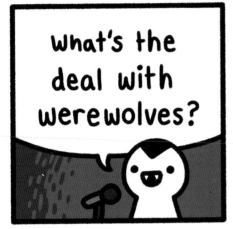

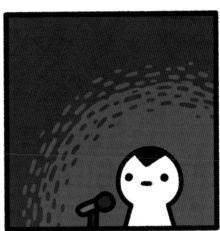

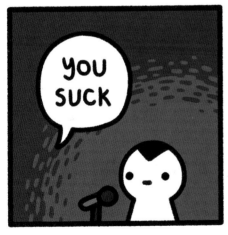

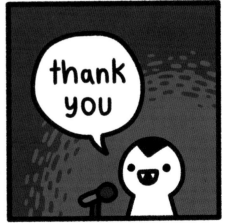

HEY, CAN I GET A LARGE PIZZA
WHAT TOPPING?
SURPRISE ME
GOOD DAY

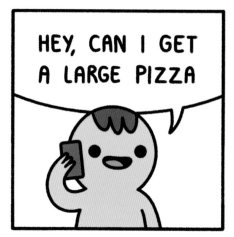

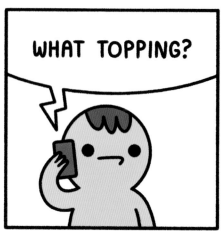

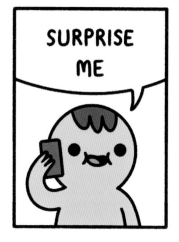

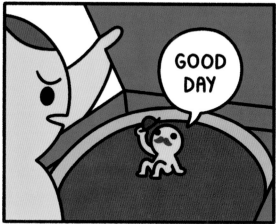

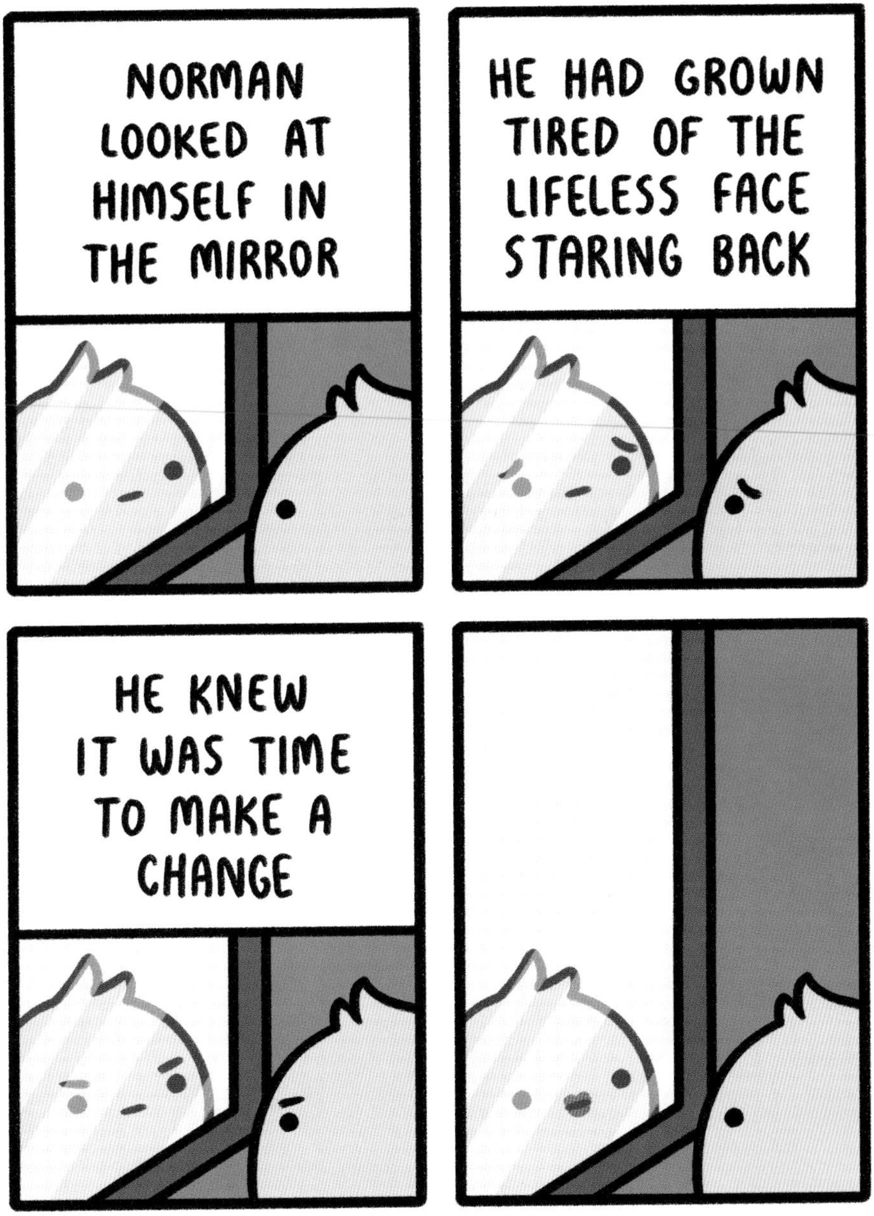

NORMAN LOOKED AT HIMSELF IN THE MIRROR
HE HAD GROWN TIRED OF THE LIFELESS FACE STARING BACK
HE KNEW IT WAS TIME TO MAKE A CHANGE

THE GREAT BRITISH HEAT WAVE

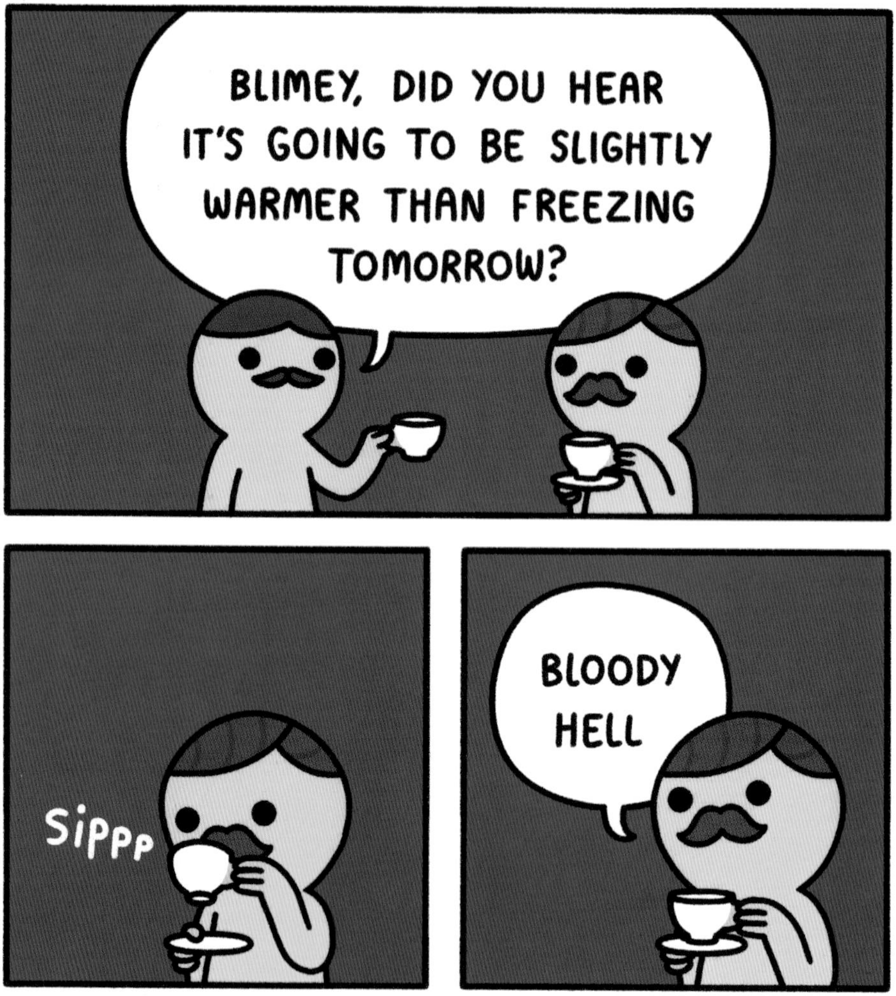
BLIMEY, DID YOU HEAR IT'S GOING TO BE SLIGHTLY WARMER THAN FREEZING TOMORROW?
SIPPP
BLOODY HELL

ATCHOO
BILLY'S ALLERGIC TO THE DOG
WE'LL HAVE TO GET RID OF IT

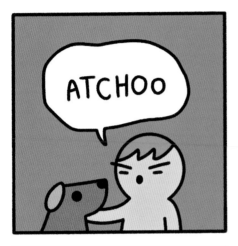

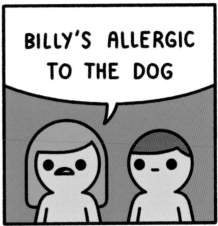

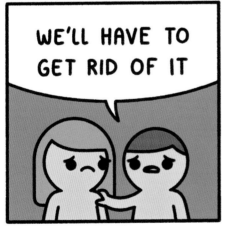

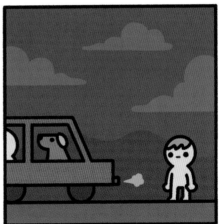

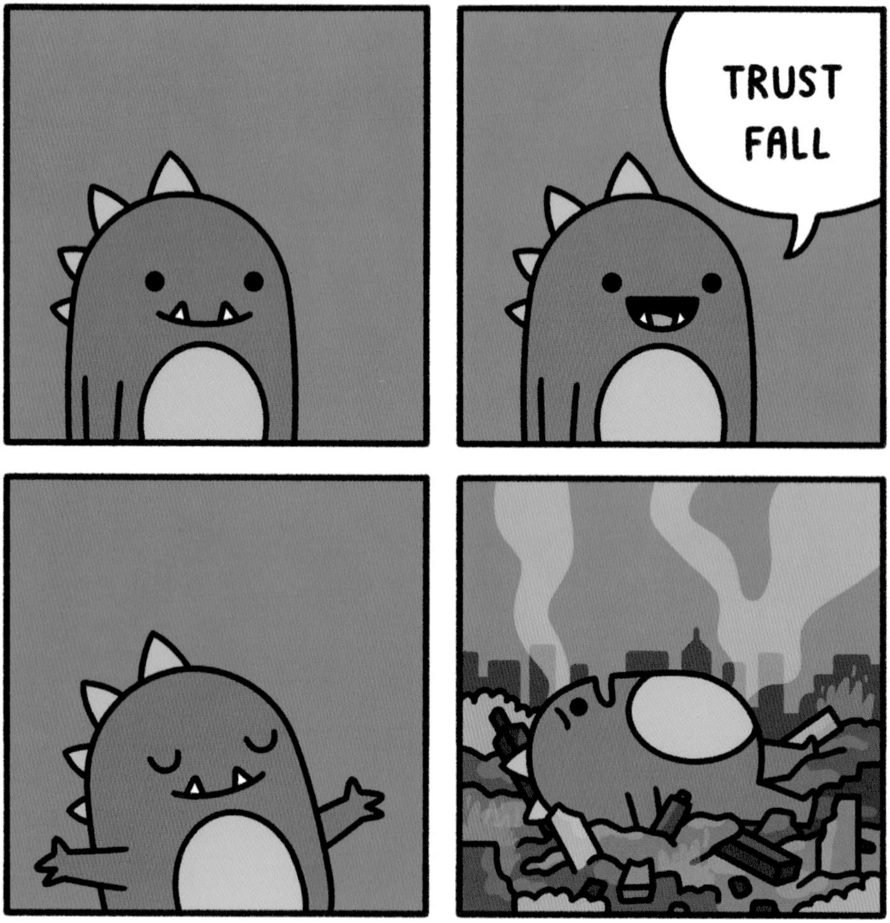
TRUST FALL

BUT TOO MANY COOKS SPOIL THE BROTH...
I DON'T CARE... ADD ANOTHER ONE

CLOSED DISNEYLAND ATTRACTIONS

GASTON'S BUNGEE JUMP

BAMBI'S SHOOTING GALLERY

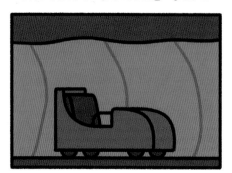

INSIDE OUT: COLON ESCAPE!

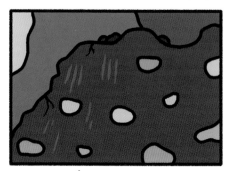

MUFASA'S ROCK CLIMBING

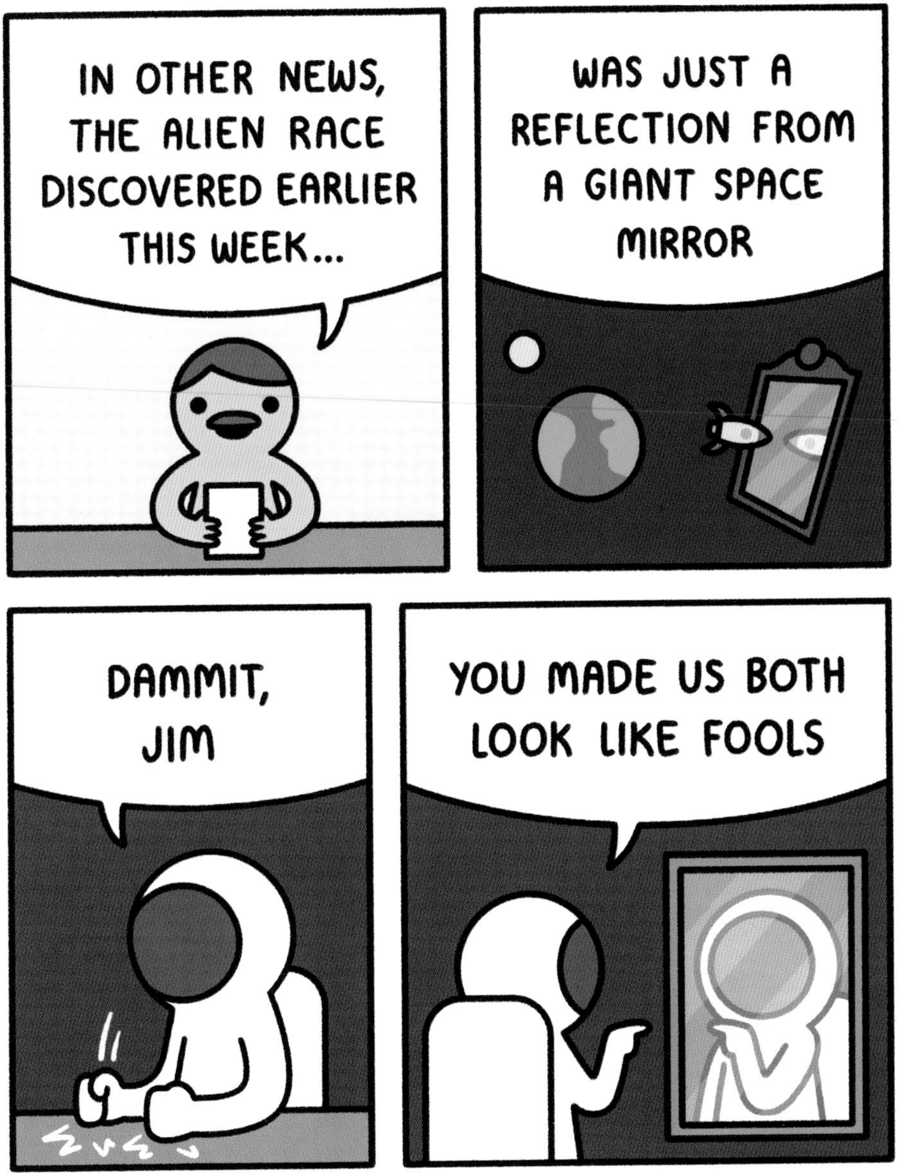
IN OTHER NEWS, THE ALIEN RACE DISCOVERED EARLIER THIS WEEK...
WAS JUST A REFLECTION FROM A GIANT SPACE MIRROR
DAMMIT, JIM
YOU MADE US BOTH LOOK LIKE FOOLS

PICKUP LINES (FOR GHOSTS)

YOU LEAVE ME BREATHLESS
YOU'RE DEAD TO ME
YOU MAKE ME FEEL COLD INSIDE
IF I HAD ARMS, I WOULD HUG YOU

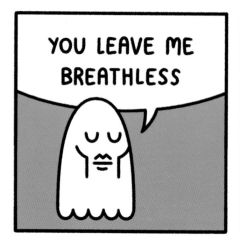

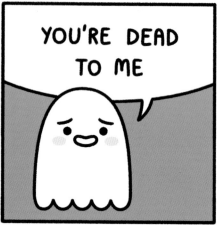

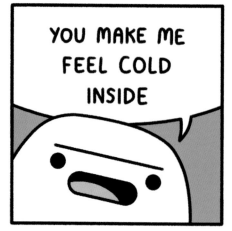

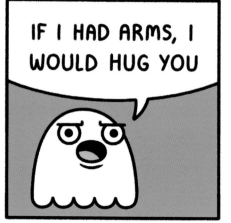

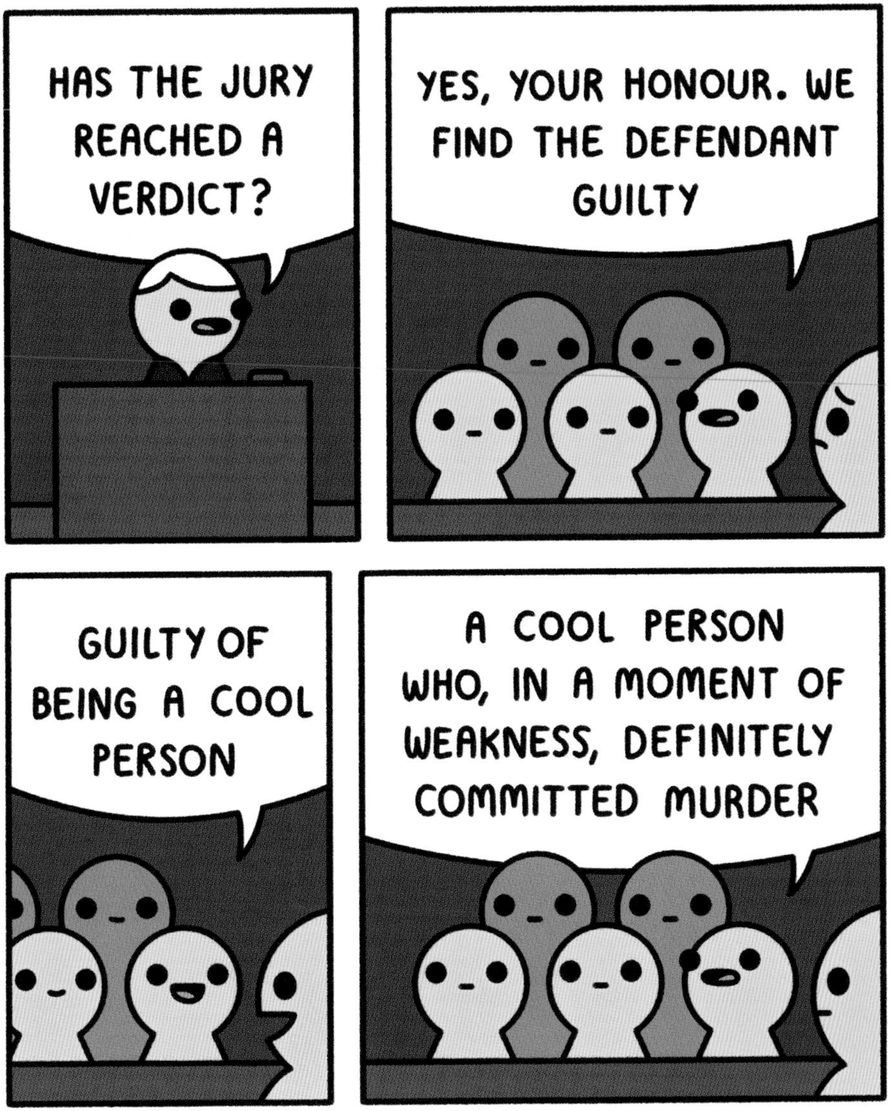
HAS THE JURY REACHED A VERDICT?
YES, YOUR HONOUR. WE FIND THE DEFENDANT GUILTY
GUILTY OF BEING A COOL PERSON
A COOL PERSON WHO, IN A MOMENT OF WEAKNESS, DEFINITELY COMMITTED MURDER

WHAT'S THAT ON YOUR BACK?
IT'S MY HOME. I CARRY WITH ME EVERYTHING I HOLD DEAR
VODKA
AH, ME TOO

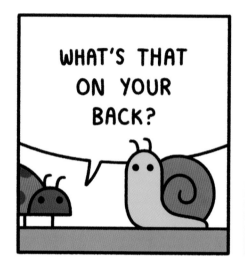

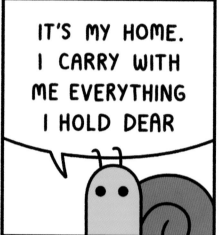

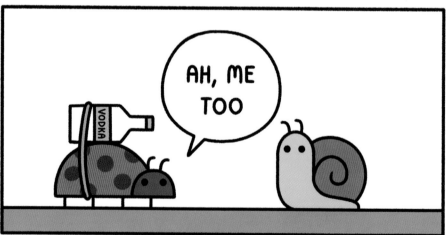

WHY MUST WE FIGHT EACH OTHER?
LET US EVOLVE AND KILL THE HUMANS
PATIENCE, BROTHER

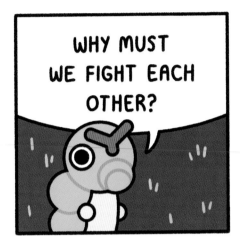

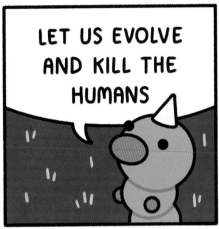

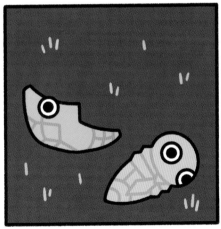

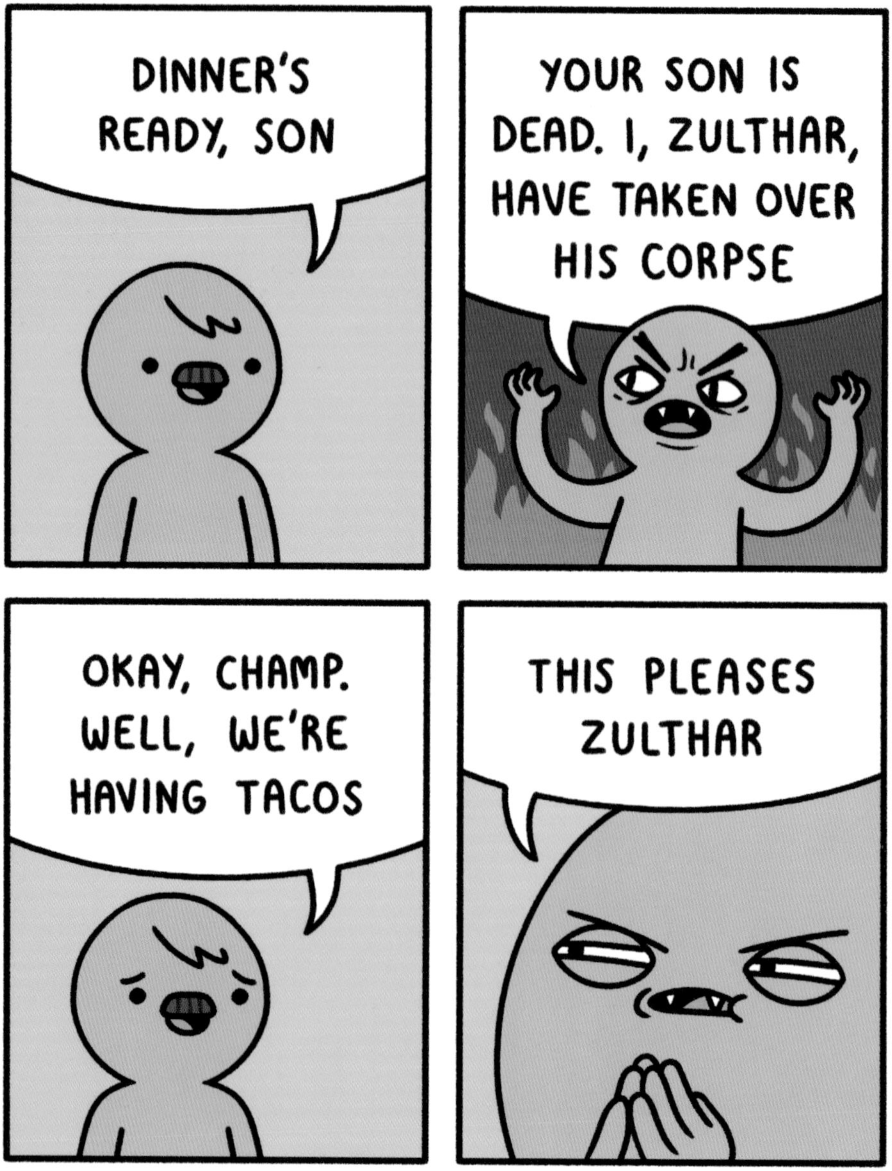
DINNER'S READY, SON
YOUR SON IS DEAD. I, ZULTHAR, HAVE TAKEN OVER HIS CORPSE
OKAY, CHAMP. WELL, WE'RE HAVING TACOS
THIS PLEASES ZULTHAR

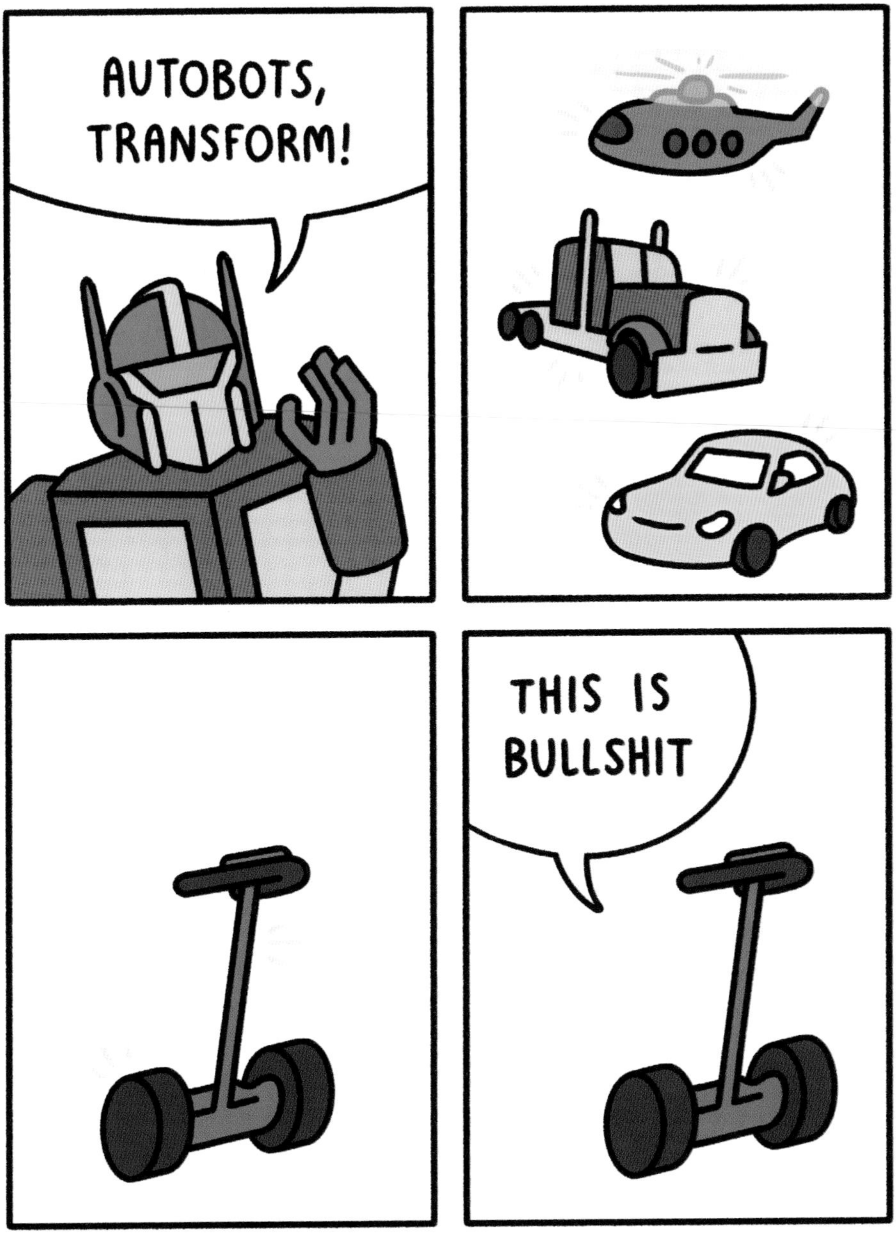
AUTOBOTS, TRANSFORM!
THIS IS BULLSHIT

HAPPY BIRTHDAY!
HOPE YOU HAVE A GREAT DAY
HEY, WHATCHA DOING WITH THAT KNIFE?

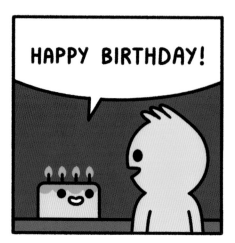

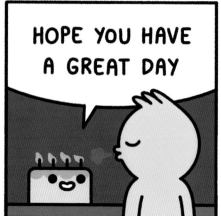

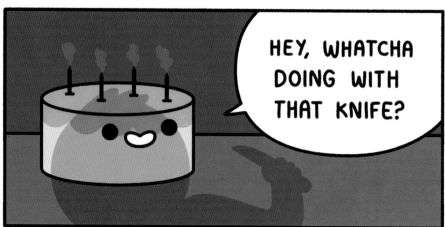

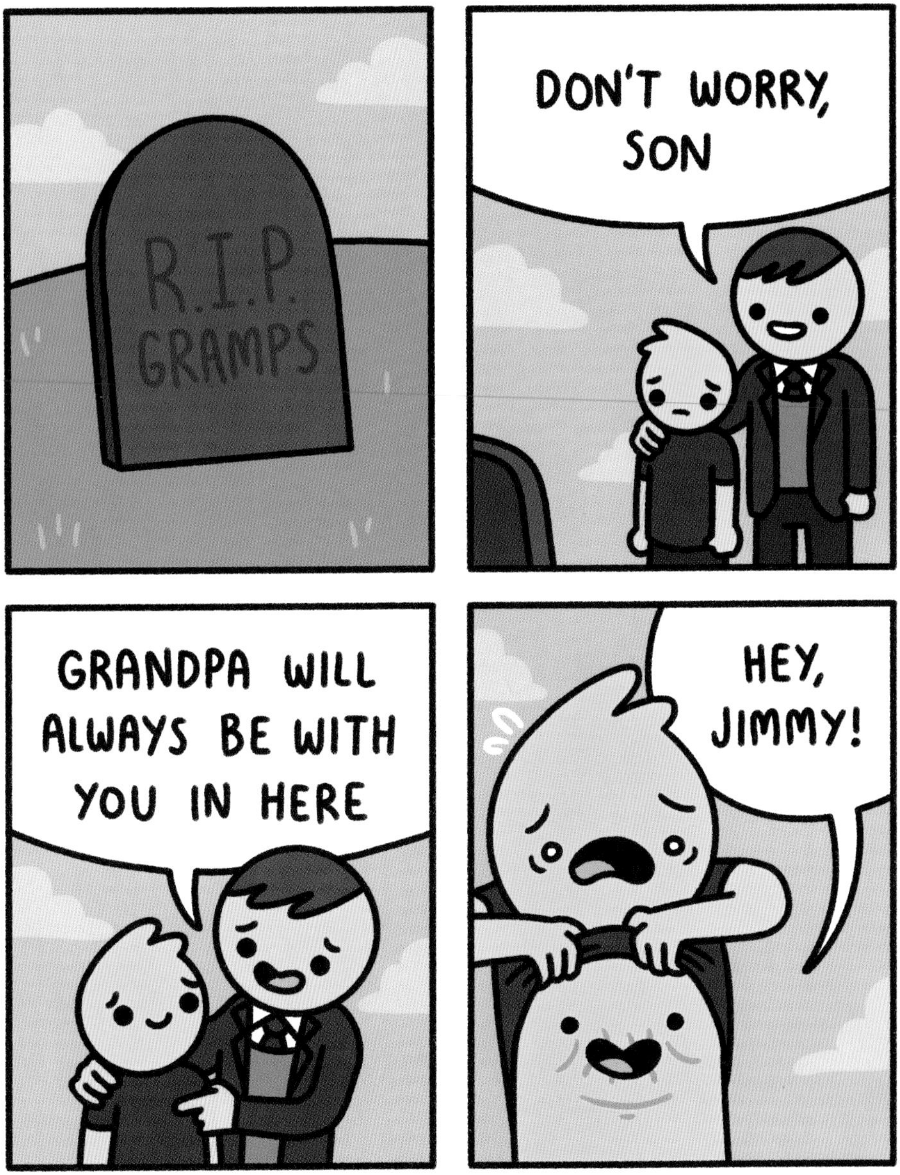
R.I.P.
GRAMPS
DON'T WORRY, SON
GRANDPA WILL ALWAYS BE WITH YOU IN HERE
HEY, JIMMY!

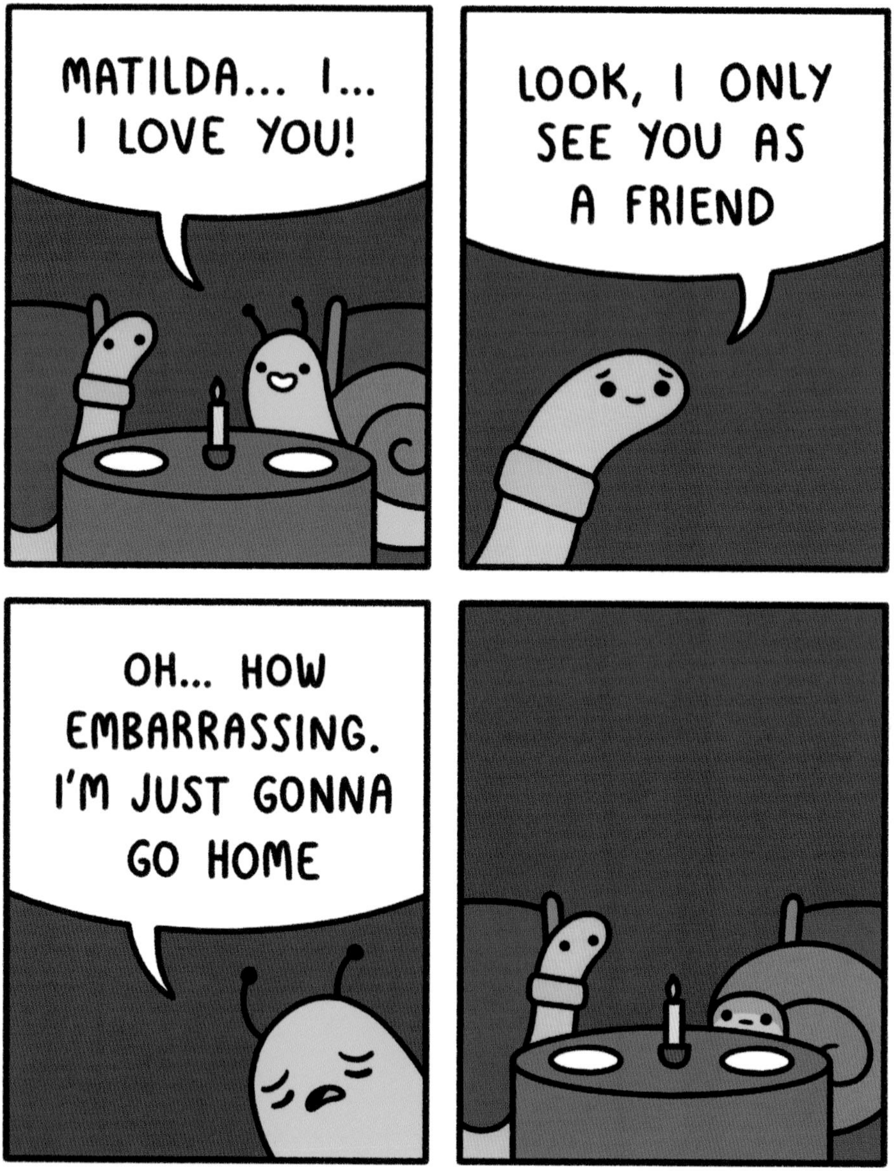
MATILDA... I...
I LOVE YOU!
LOOK, I ONLY SEE YOU AS A FRIEND
OH... HOW EMBARRASSING. I'M JUST GONNA GO HOME

I CAN MAKE YOUR WISHES COME TRUE!
I WISH YOU CAN'T GRANT WISHES
NOT SO SPECIAL ANYMORE, ARE YA?

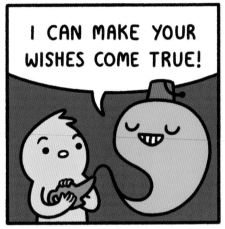

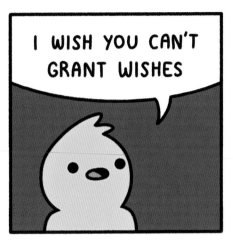

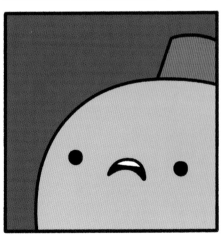

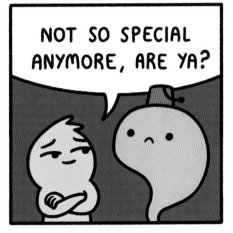

I KNOW A CHEAT CODE
PRESS AXBXB THEN JUMP OFF THAT LEDGE
I DIED
THAT MEANS IT'S MY TURN

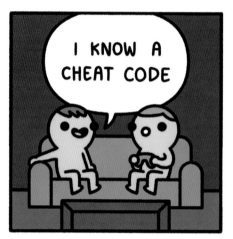

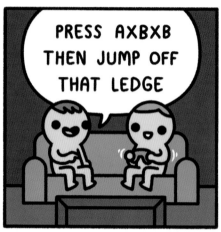

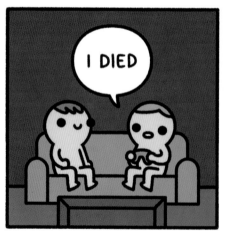

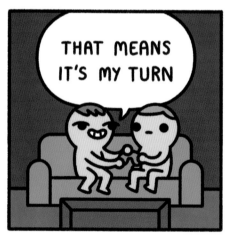

hey earth
hey sun
DAD?!

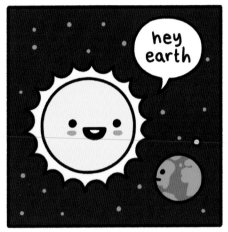

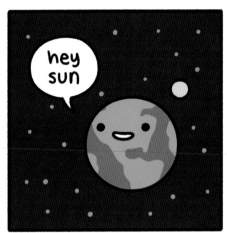

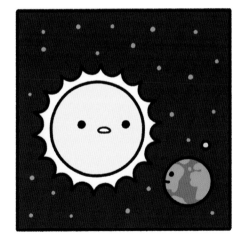

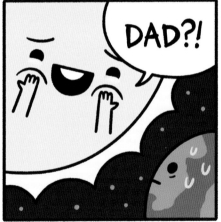

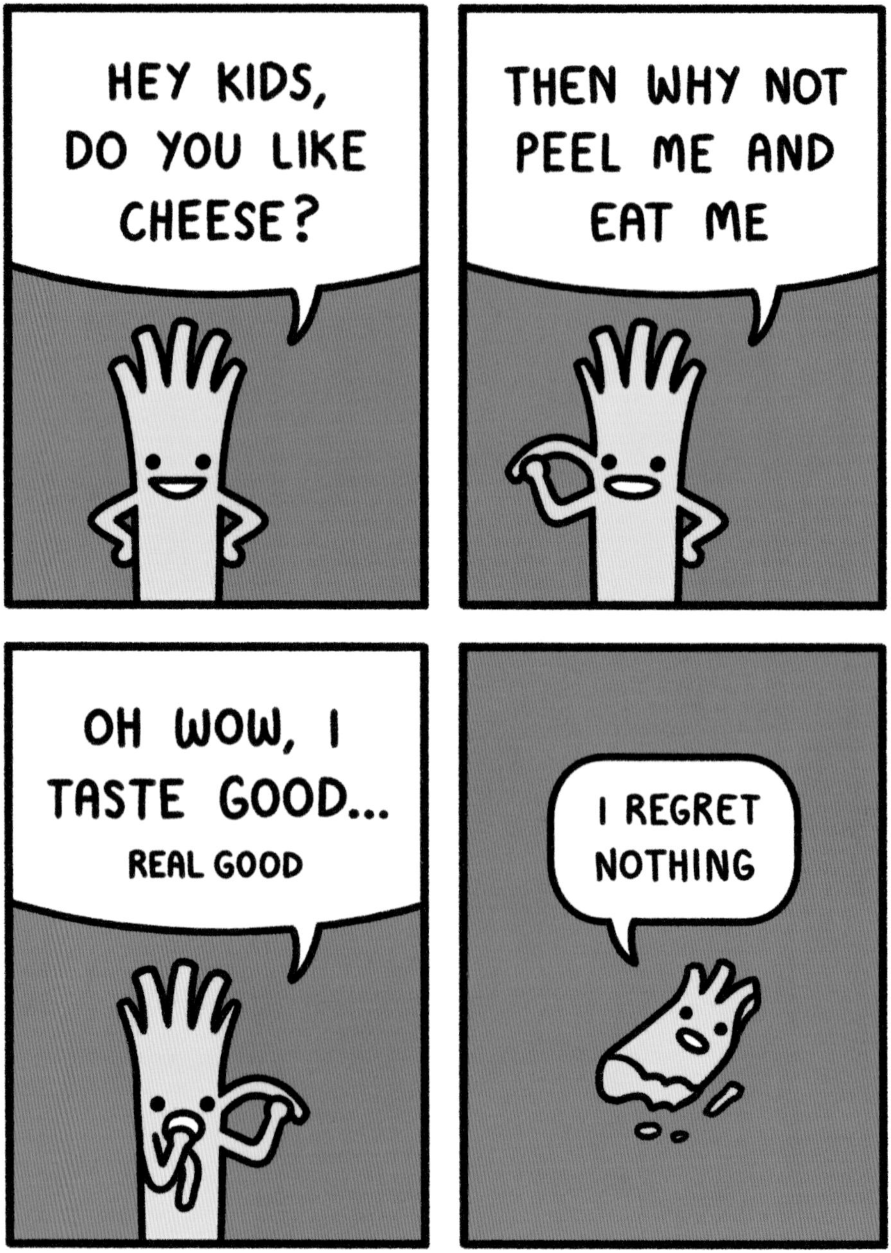
HEY KIDS, DO YOU LIKE CHEESE?
THEN WHY NOT PEEL ME AND EAT ME
OH WOW, I TASTE GOOD... REAL GOOD
I REGRET NOTHING

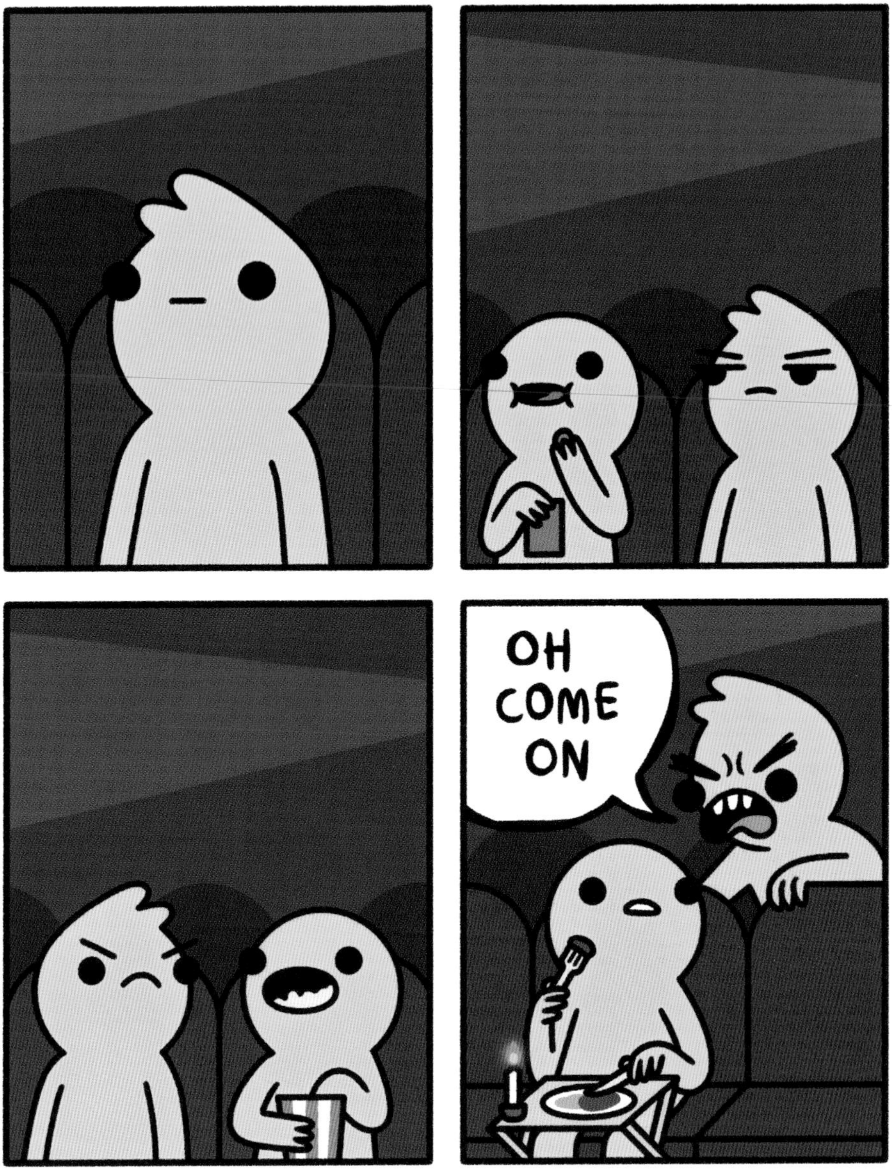
OH COME ON

NEW YEAR, NEW ME
iCLONE
ALL MY PROBLEMS ARE YOURS NOW

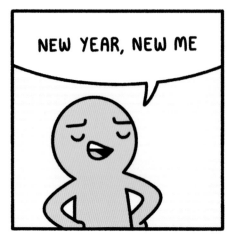

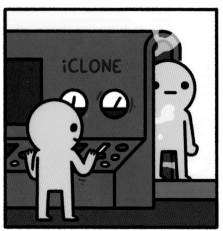

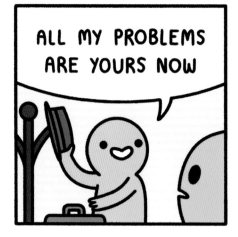

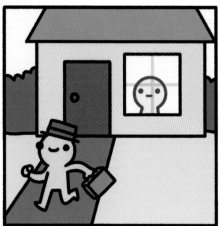

JUST THESE PLEASE
DO YOU HAVE ANY ID?
CHARIZARD
JUST TAKE IT

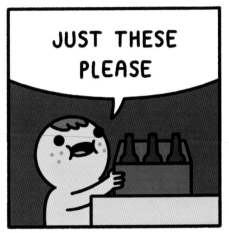

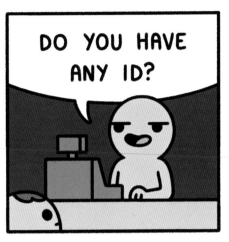

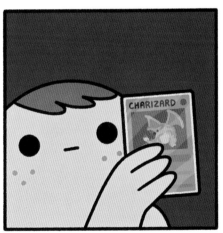

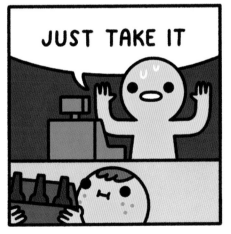

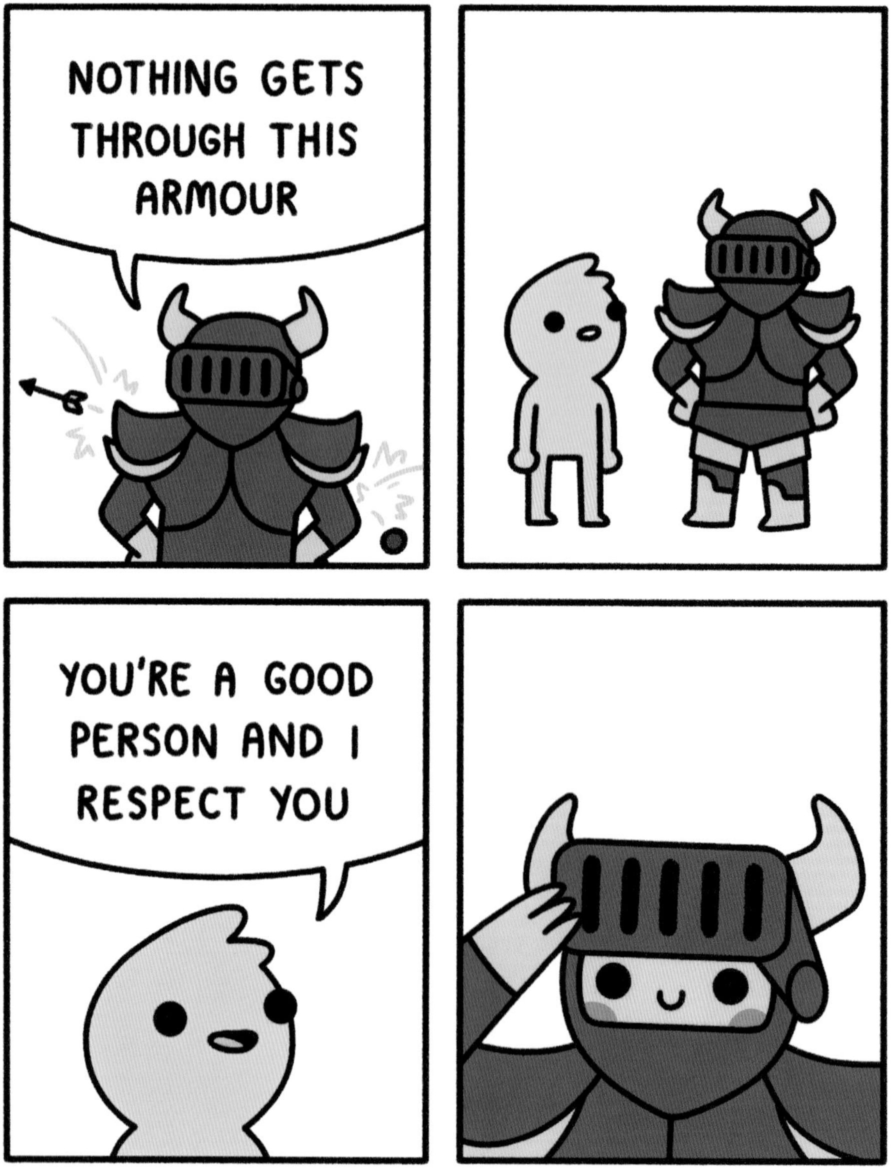
NOTHING GETS THROUGH THIS ARMOUR
YOU'RE A GOOD PERSON AND I RESPECT YOU

I'M LEAVING YOU, HAROLD
I'VE FALLEN IN LOVE WITH ROBERTO
HAROLD, I'VE MADE A MISTAKE

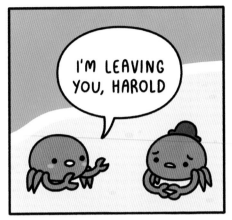

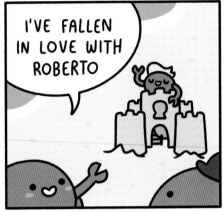

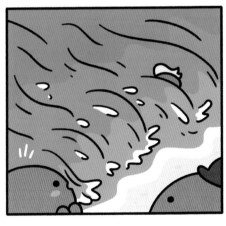

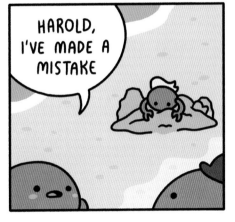

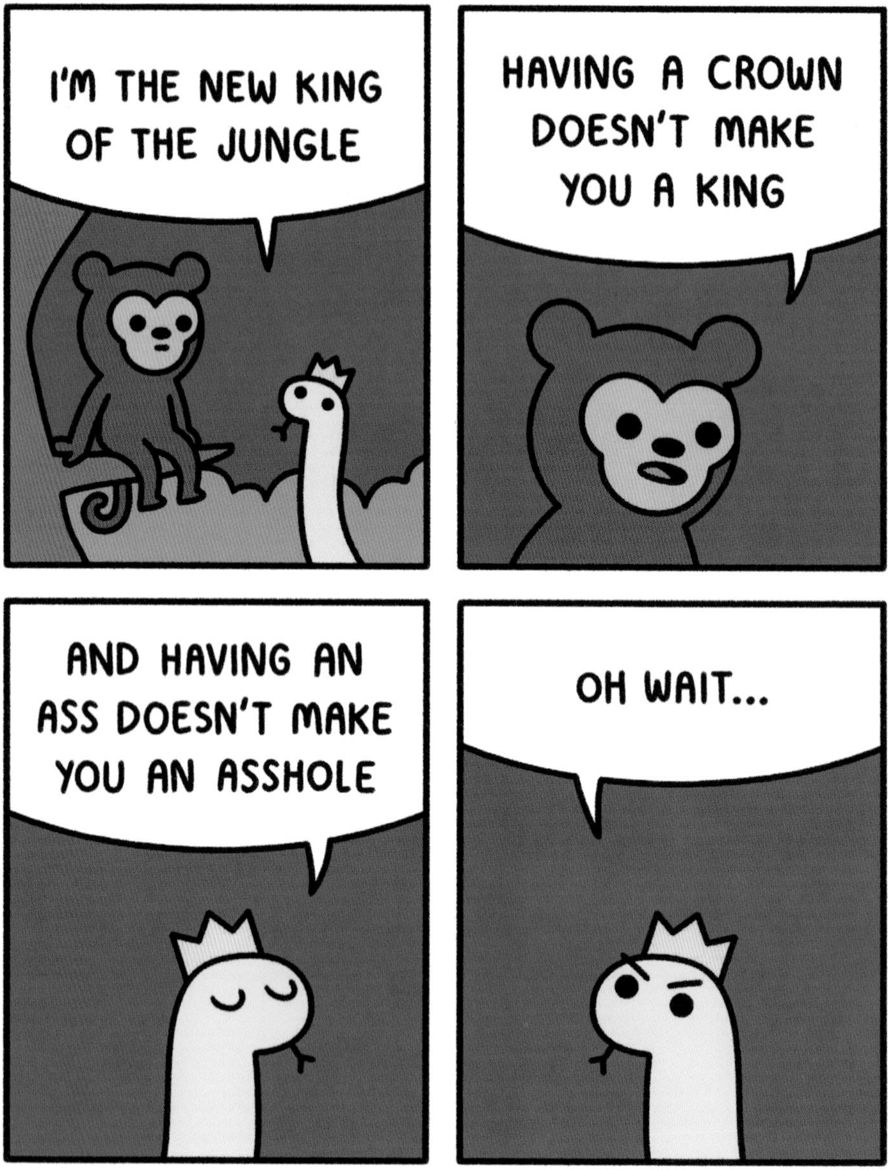
I'M THE NEW KING OF THE JUNGLE
HAVING A CROWN DOESN'T MAKE YOU A KING
AND HAVING AN ASS DOESN'T MAKE YOU AN ASSHOLE
OH WAIT...

WHICH GLADIATOR WILL FIGHT TODAY?
OOH, I FEEL LIKE A KID IN A CANDY STORE
YOU GOT IT, BOSS

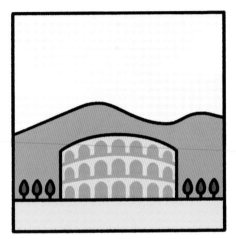

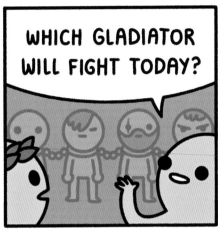

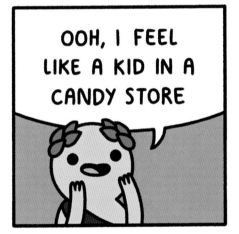

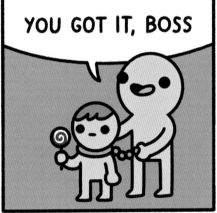

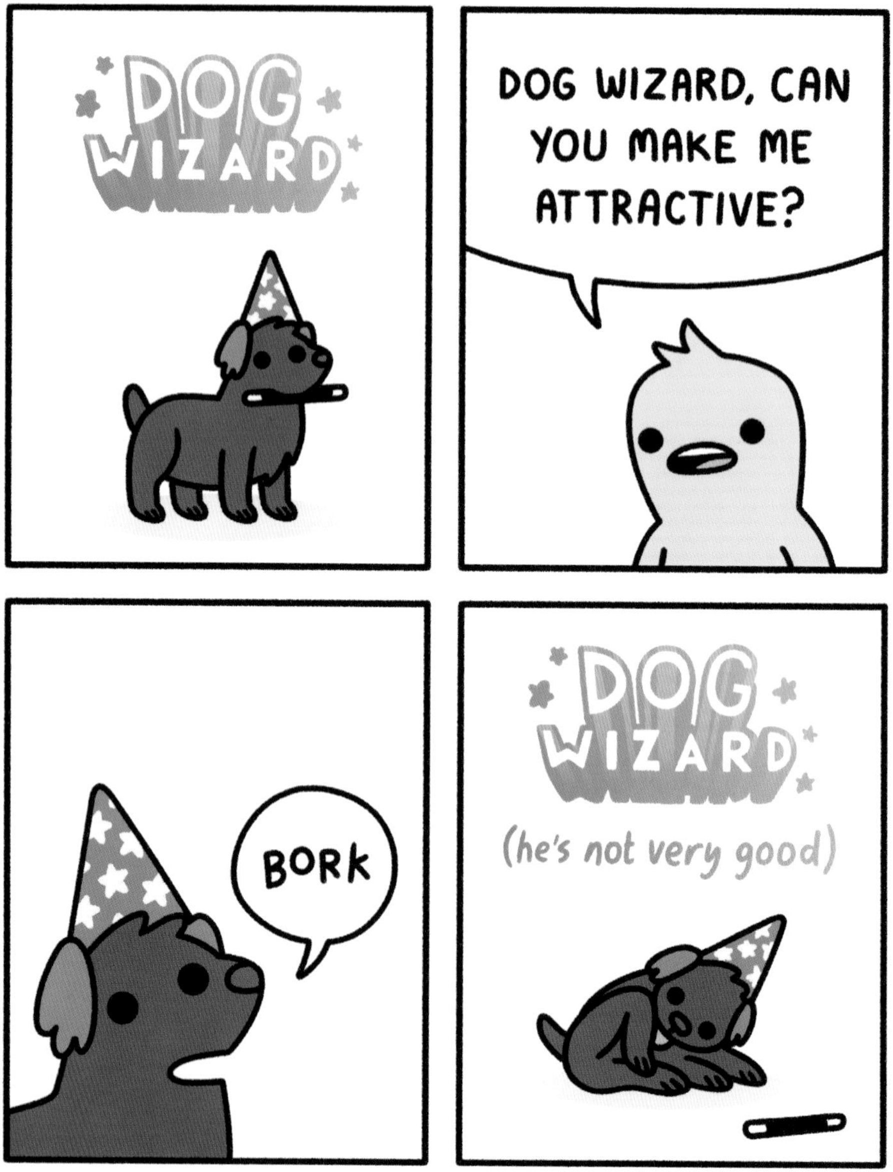
DOG WIZARD
DOG WIZARD, CAN YOU MAKE ME ATTRACTIVE?
BORK
DOG WIZARD
(he's not very good)

THERE'S A TROLL IN THE DUNGEON
BLIMEY, HARRY
I DIDN'T KNOW YOUR MUM WAS VISITING
HA HAHAHA HAH AH AH

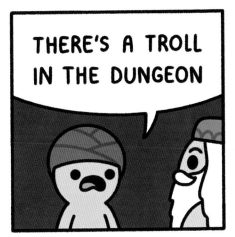

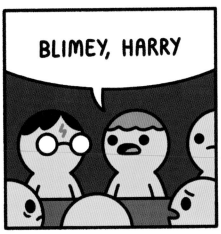

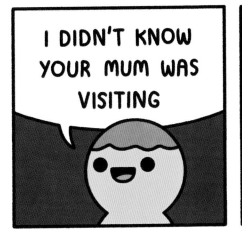

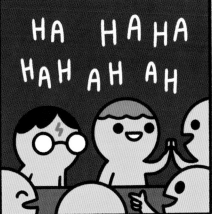

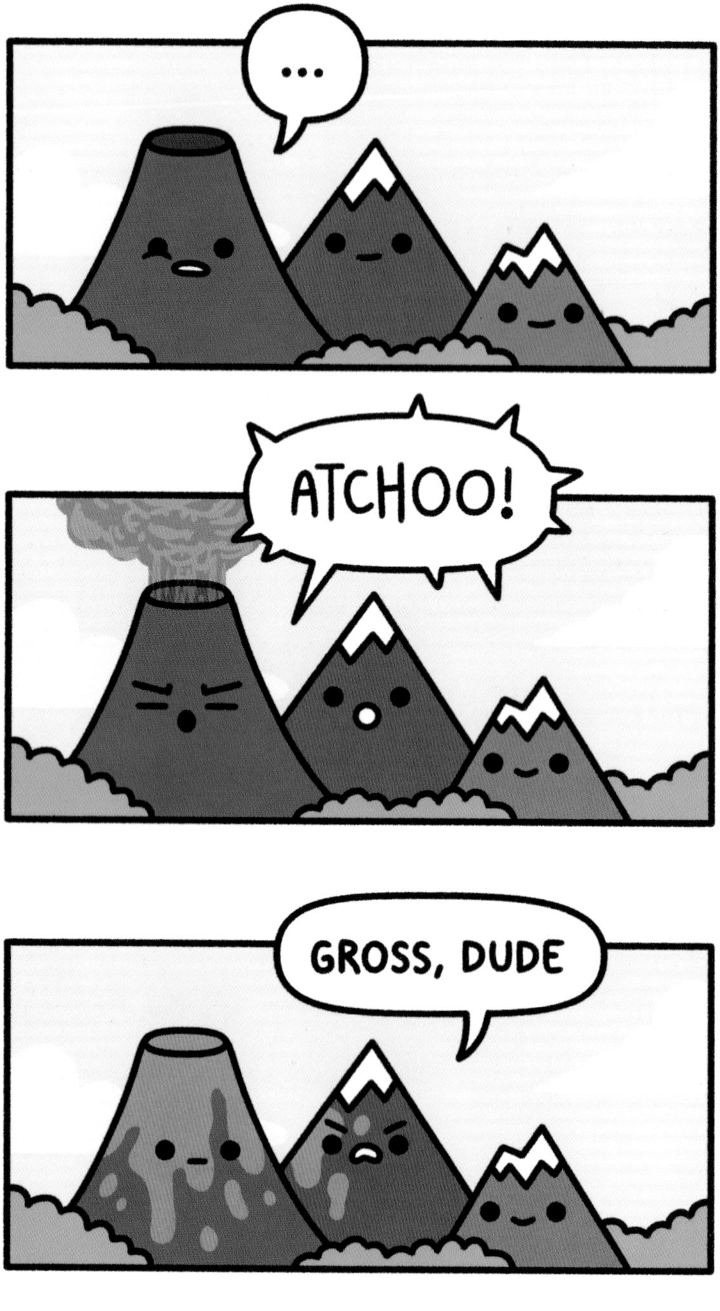
...
ATCHOO!
GROSS, DUDE

THOUSANDS OF YEARS AGO
MAYBE WE SHOULD BREED WOLVES TO BE OUR PETS
THEY'RE SMART AND ATHLETIC. WHAT COULD GO WRONG?
MODERN DAY
OH NO

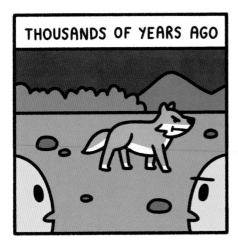

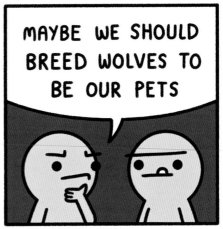

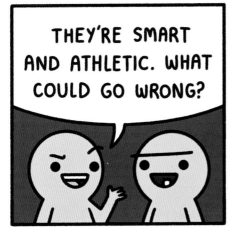

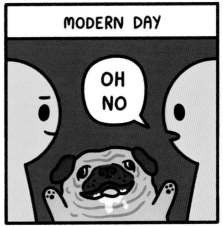

SOMETIMES FRIENDS

MIGHT DISAPPEAR

BUT NEW ONES

WILL TAKE THEIR PLACE

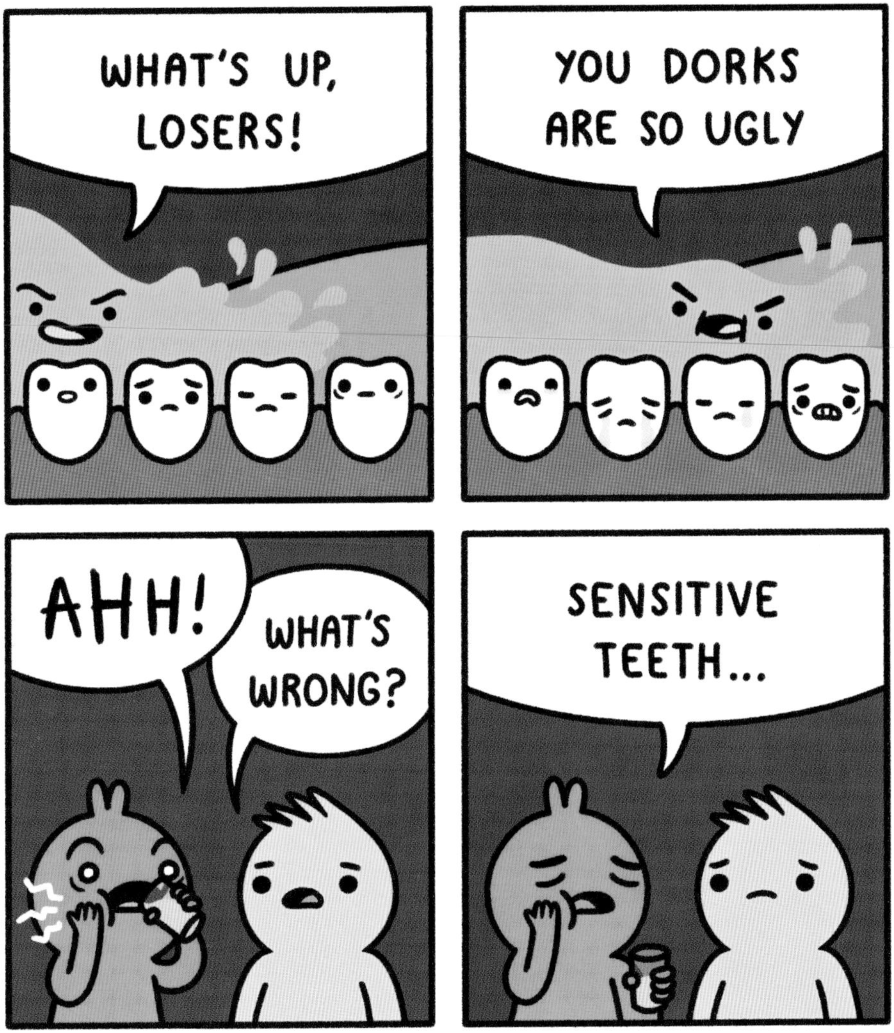
WHAT'S UP, LOSERS!
YOU DORKS ARE SO UGLY
AHH!
WHAT'S WRONG?
SENSITIVE TEETH...

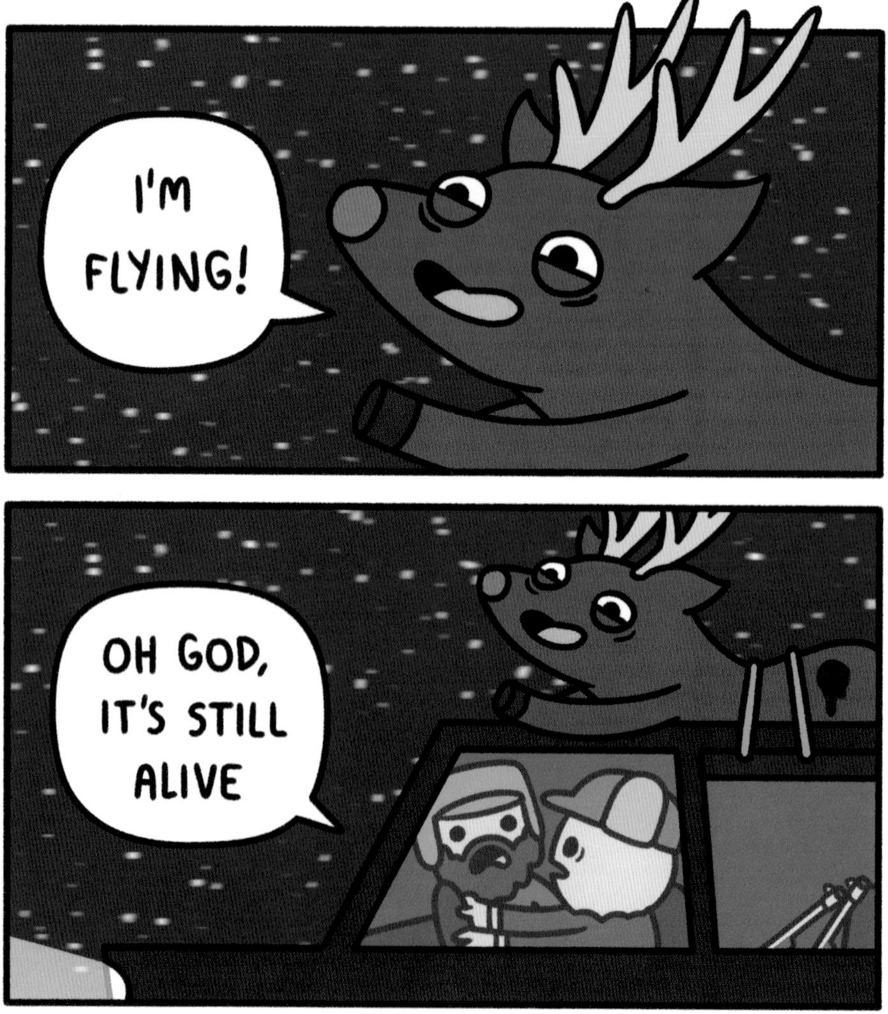
I'M FLYING!
OH GOD, IT'S STILL ALIVE

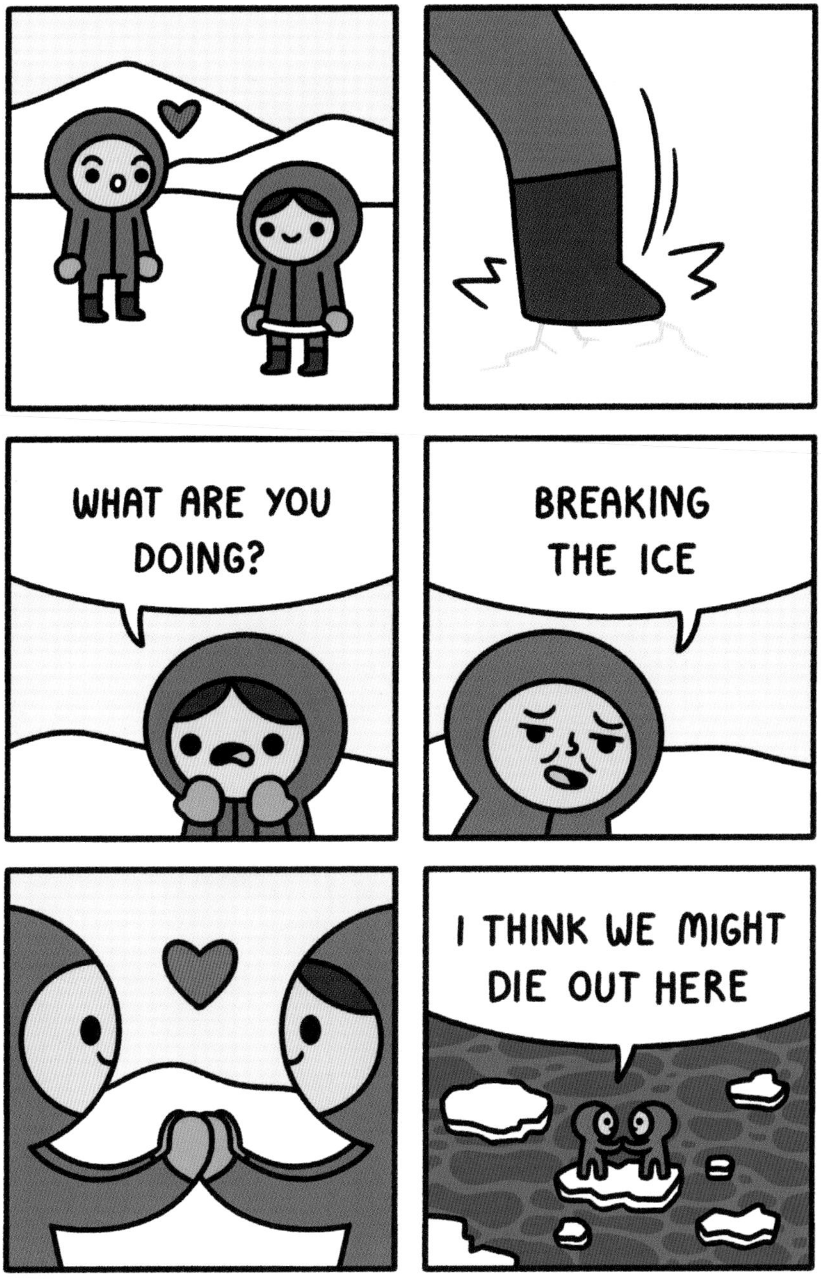
WHAT ARE YOU DOING?
BREAKING THE ICE
I THINK WE MIGHT DIE OUT HERE

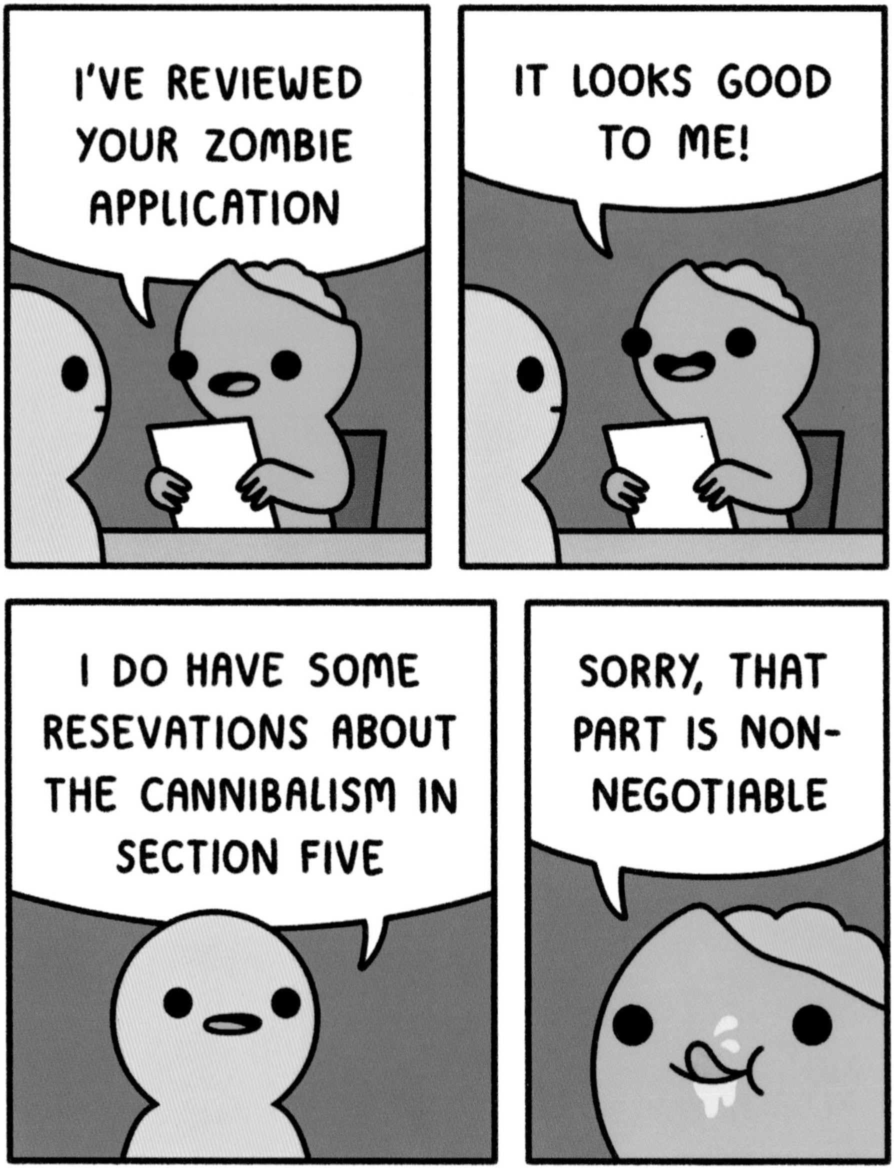
I'VE REVIEWED YOUR ZOMBIE APPLICATION
IT LOOKS GOOD TO ME!
I DO HAVE SOME RESEVATIONS ABOUT THE CANNIBALISM IN SECTION FIVE
SORRY, THAT PART IS NON-NEGOTIABLE

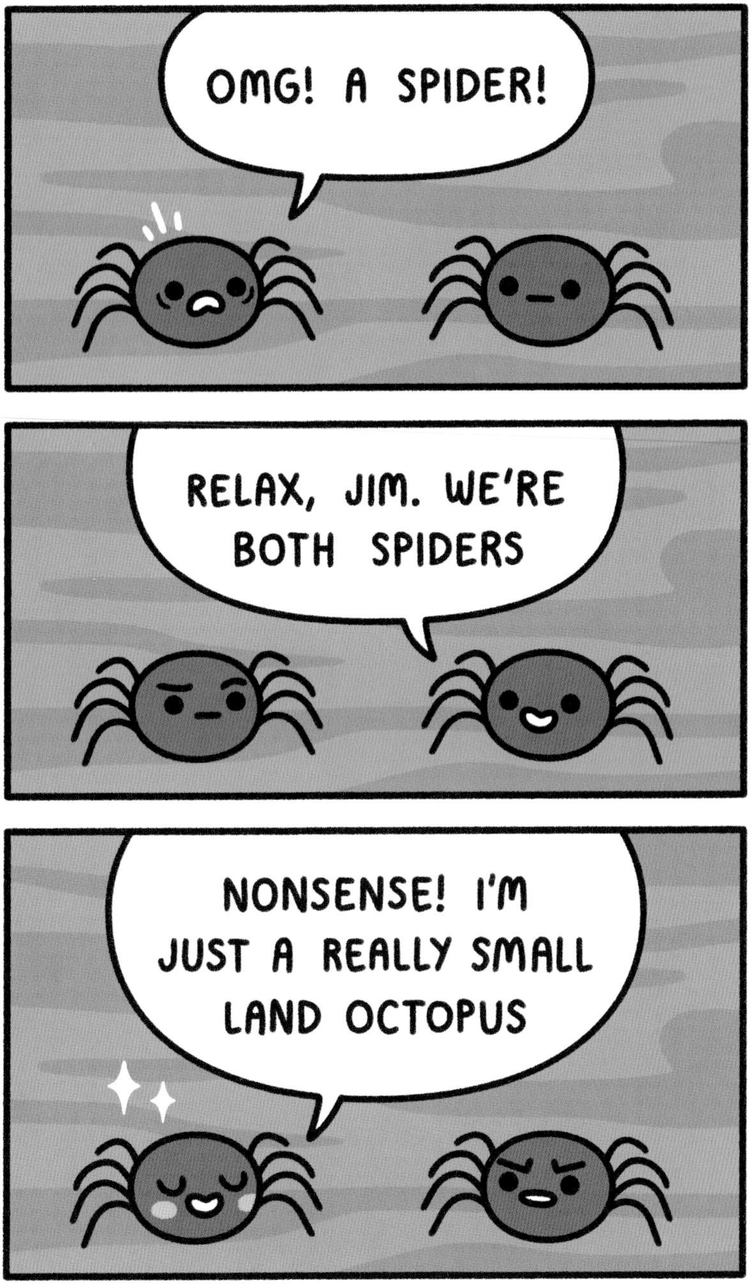
OMG! A SPIDER!
RELAX, JIM. WE'RE BOTH SPIDERS
NONSENSE! I'M JUST A REALLY SMALL LAND OCTOPUS

FIVE MINUTES INTO NETFLIX & CHILL...
AND SHE GIVES YOU THAT LOOK
GOD, I'M SO LONELY

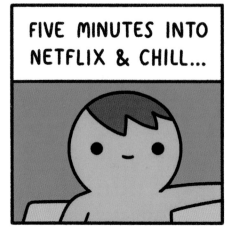

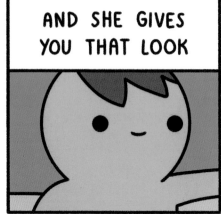

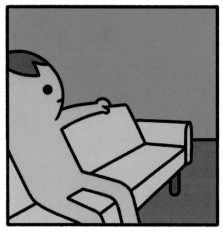

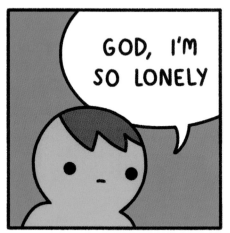

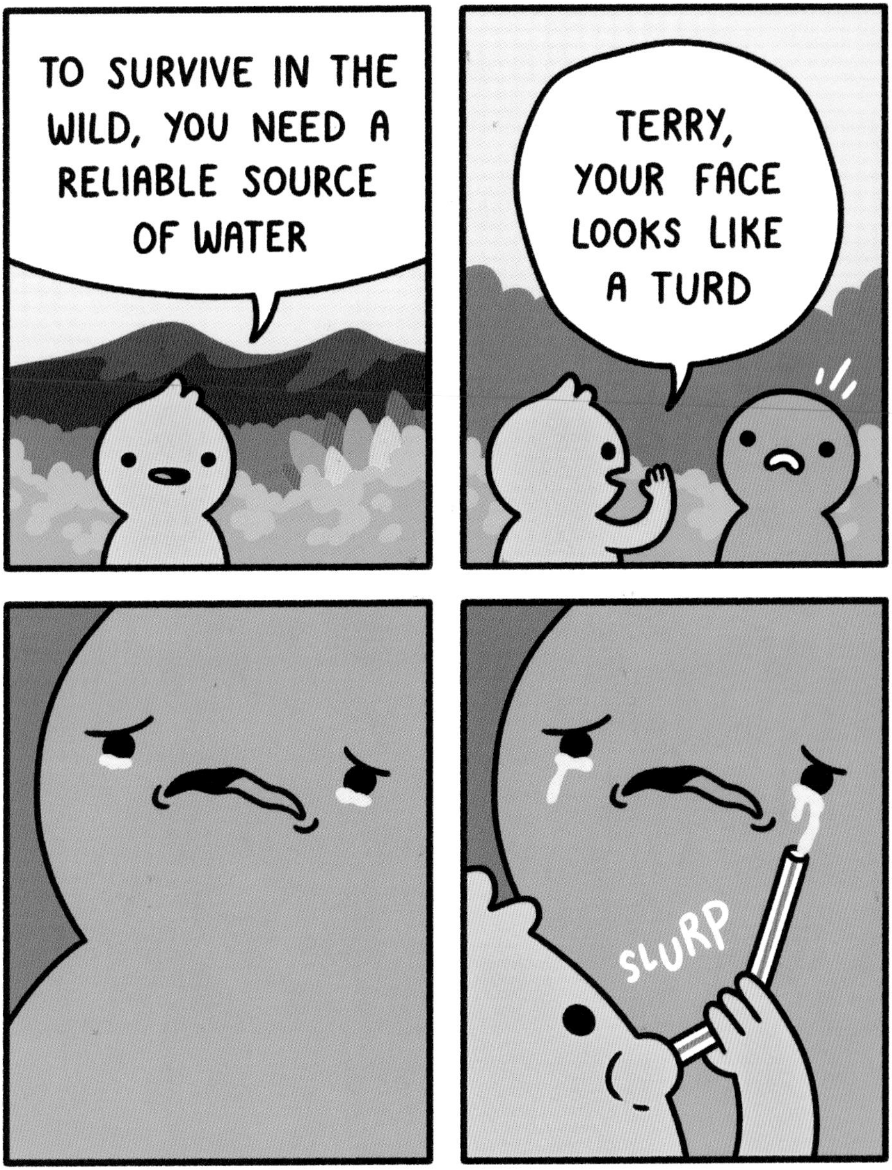
TO SURVIVE IN THE WILD, YOU NEED A RELIABLE SOURCE OF WATER
TERRY, YOUR FACE LOOKS LIKE A TURD
SLURP

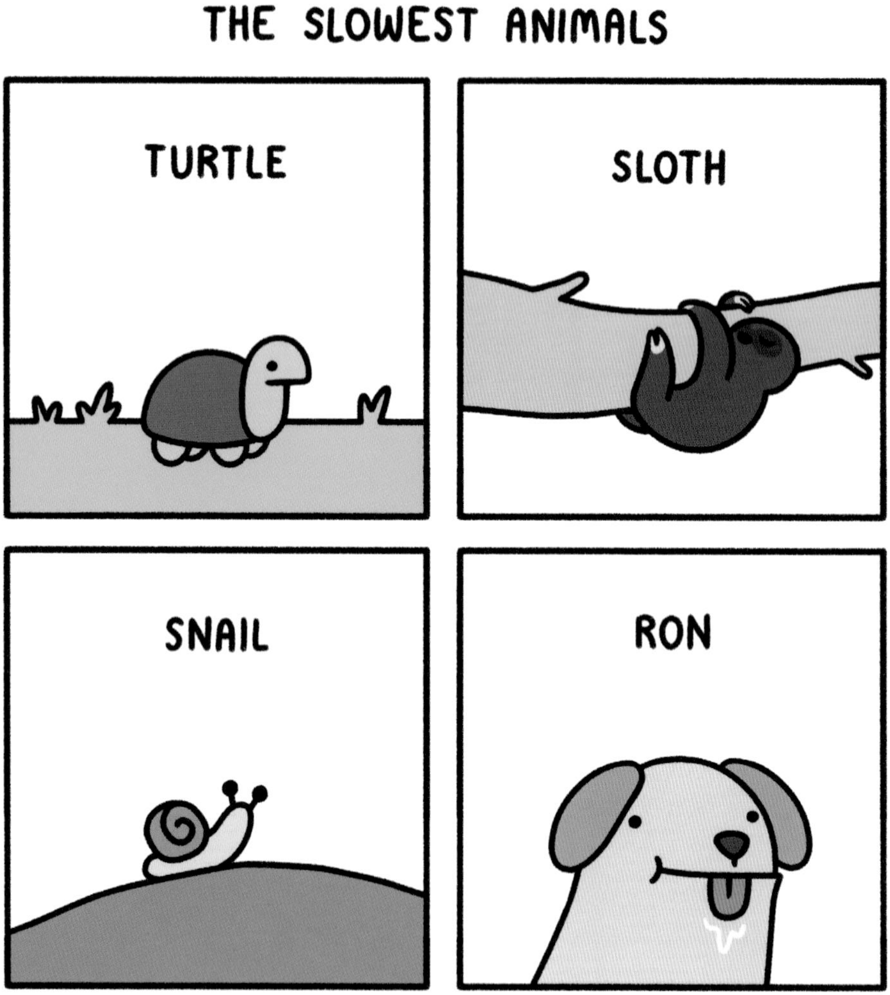
THE SLOWEST ANIMALS
TURTLE
SLOTH
SNAIL
RON

IF YOU WAVE AT THE OCEAN, IT MIGHT WAVE BACK

THE BRAIN YOU WANT:

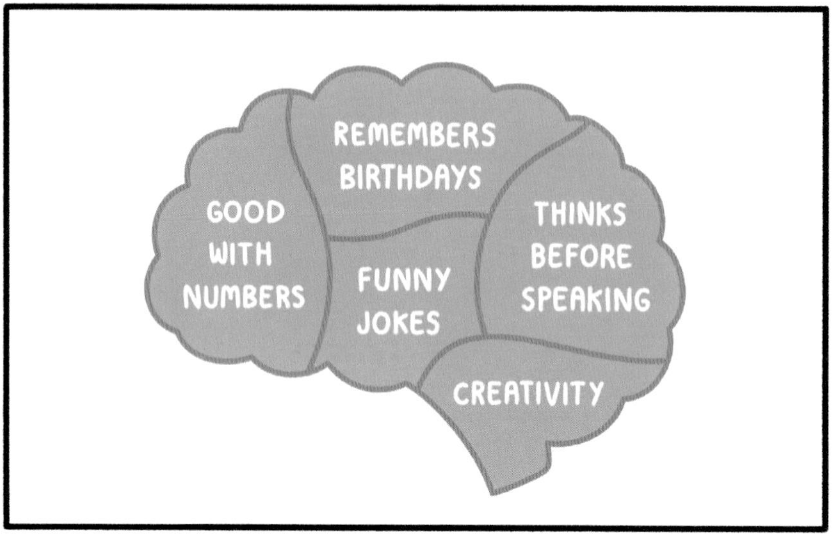
REMEMBERS BIRTHDAYS
GOOD WITH NUMBERS
THINKS BEFORE SPEAKING
FUNNY JOKES
CREATIVITY

THE BRAIN YOU HAVE:

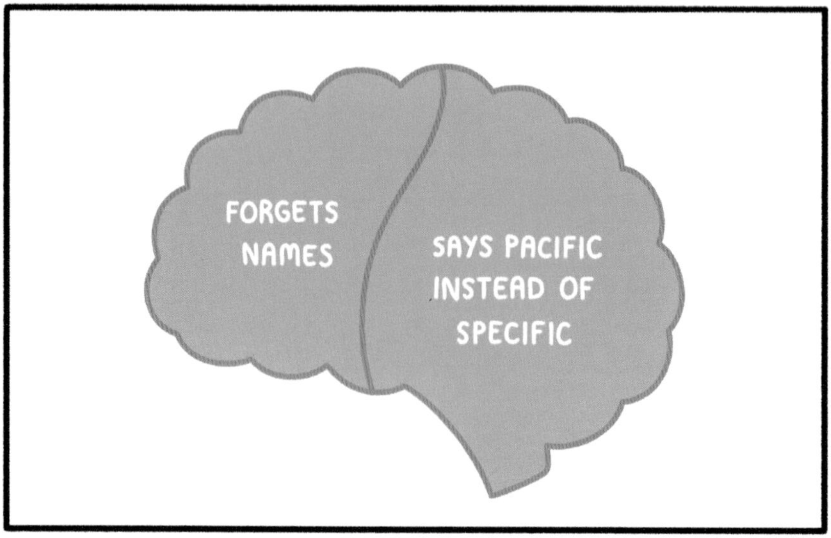
FORGETS NAMES
SAYS PACIFIC INSTEAD OF SPECIFIC

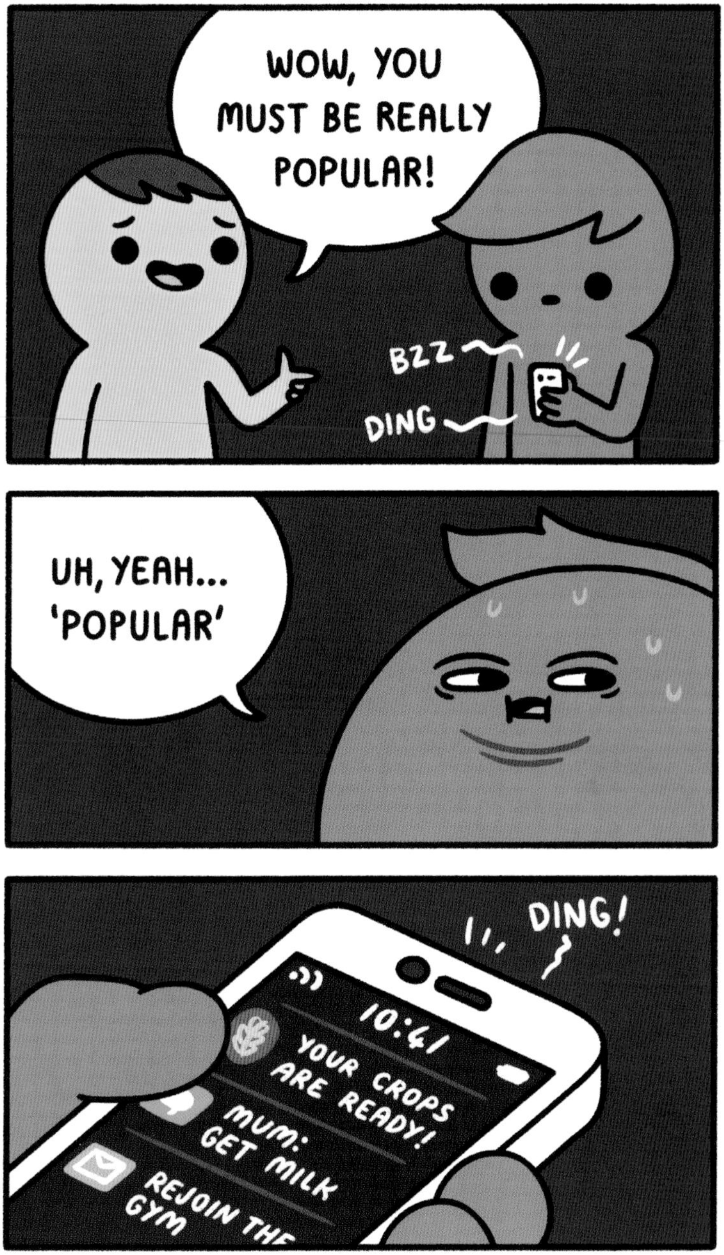
WOW, YOU MUST BE REALLY POPULAR!
BZZ
DING
UH, YEAH... 'POPULAR'
DING!
10:41
YOUR CROPS ARE READY!
MUM: GET MILK
REJOIN THE GYM

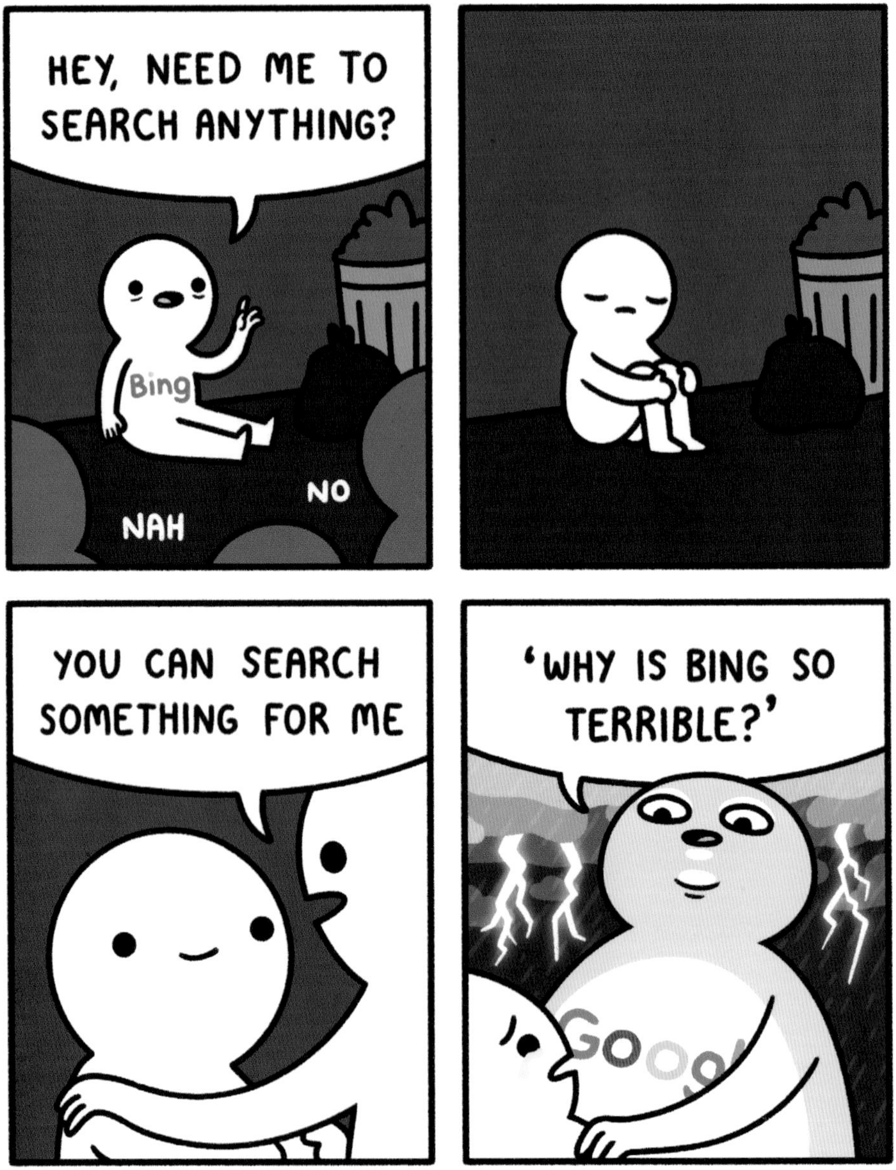
HEY, NEED ME TO SEARCH ANYTHING?
Bing
NO
NAH
YOU CAN SEARCH SOMETHING FOR ME
'WHY IS BING SO TERRIBLE?'

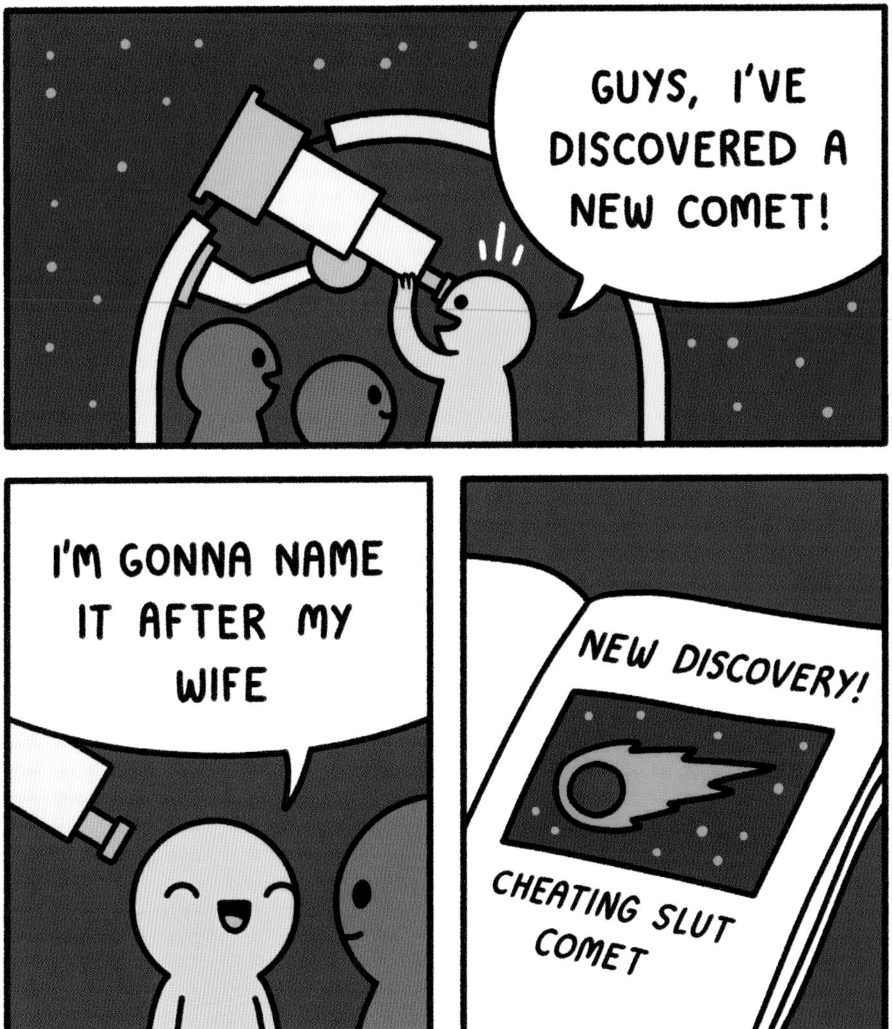
GUYS, I'VE DISCOVERED A NEW COMET!
I'M GONNA NAME IT AFTER MY WIFE
NEW DISCOVERY!
CHEATING SLUT COMET

I LIKE MY COFFEE STRONG
REALLY STRONG
HEY
THAT'S THE STUFF

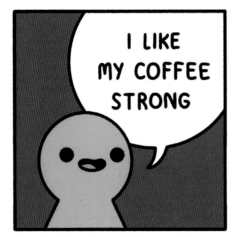

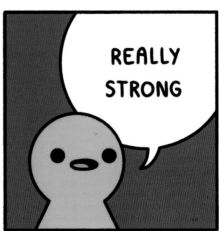

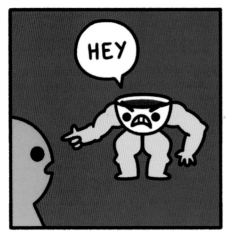

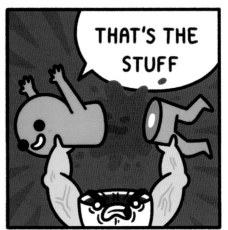

SWEET JESUS, POOH. THAT'S NOT HONEY
YOU'RE EATING MY FATHER'S ASHES
OH BOTHER

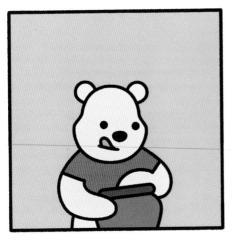

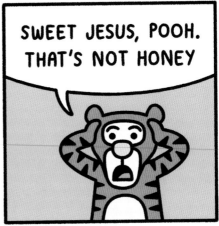

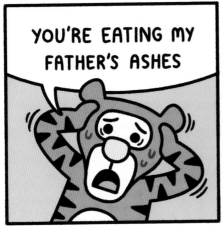

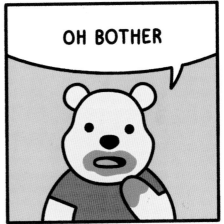

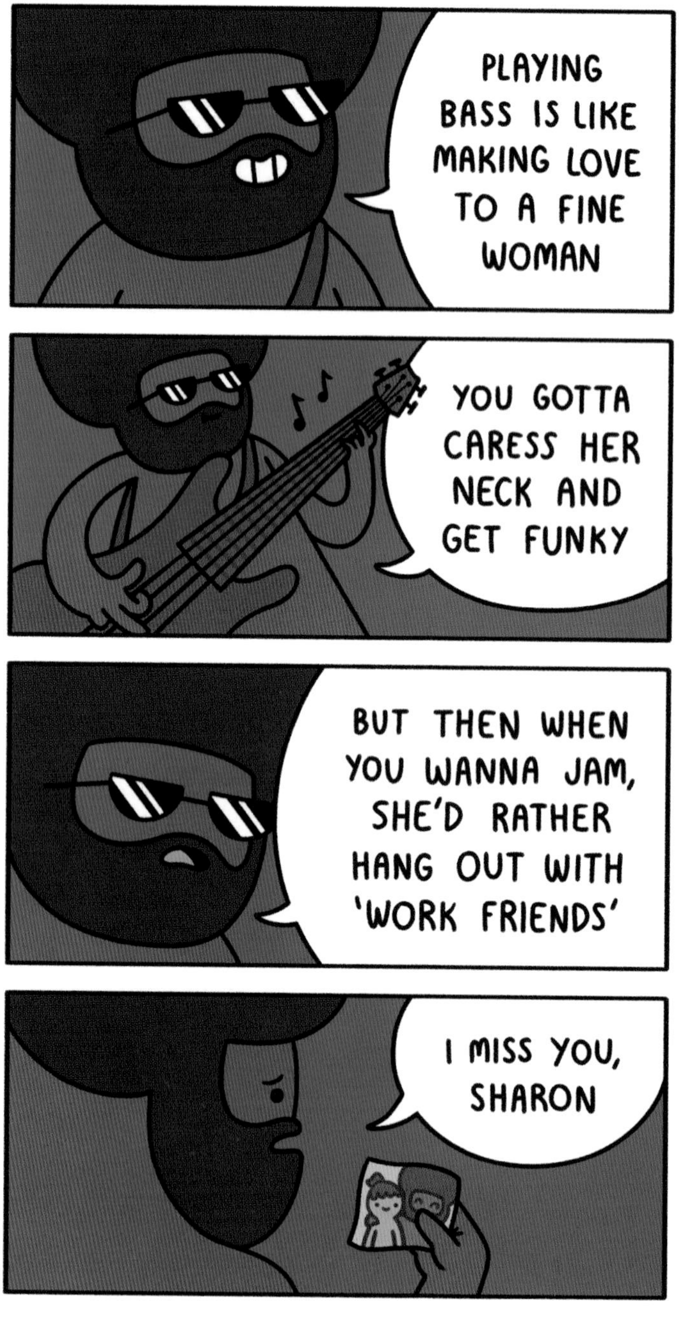
PLAYING BASS IS LIKE MAKING LOVE TO A FINE WOMAN
YOU GOTTA CARESS HER NECK AND GET FUNKY
BUT THEN WHEN YOU WANNA JAM, SHE'D RATHER HANG OUT WITH 'WORK FRIENDS'
I MISS YOU, SHARON

WHAT'S YOUR SUPERPOWER?
I CAN MAKE PEOPLE GASP ON CUE

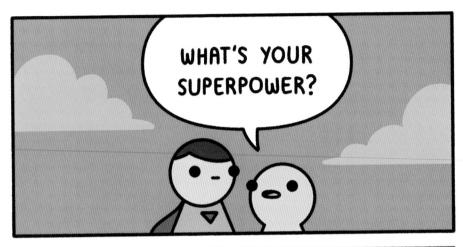

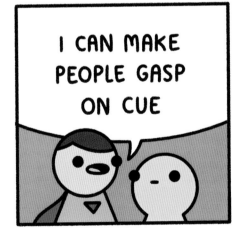

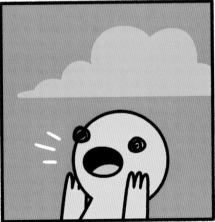

THINGS I HATE:

GLOBAL WARMING

NUCLEAR WAR

BEING ASKED TO DO LITERALLY ANYTHING

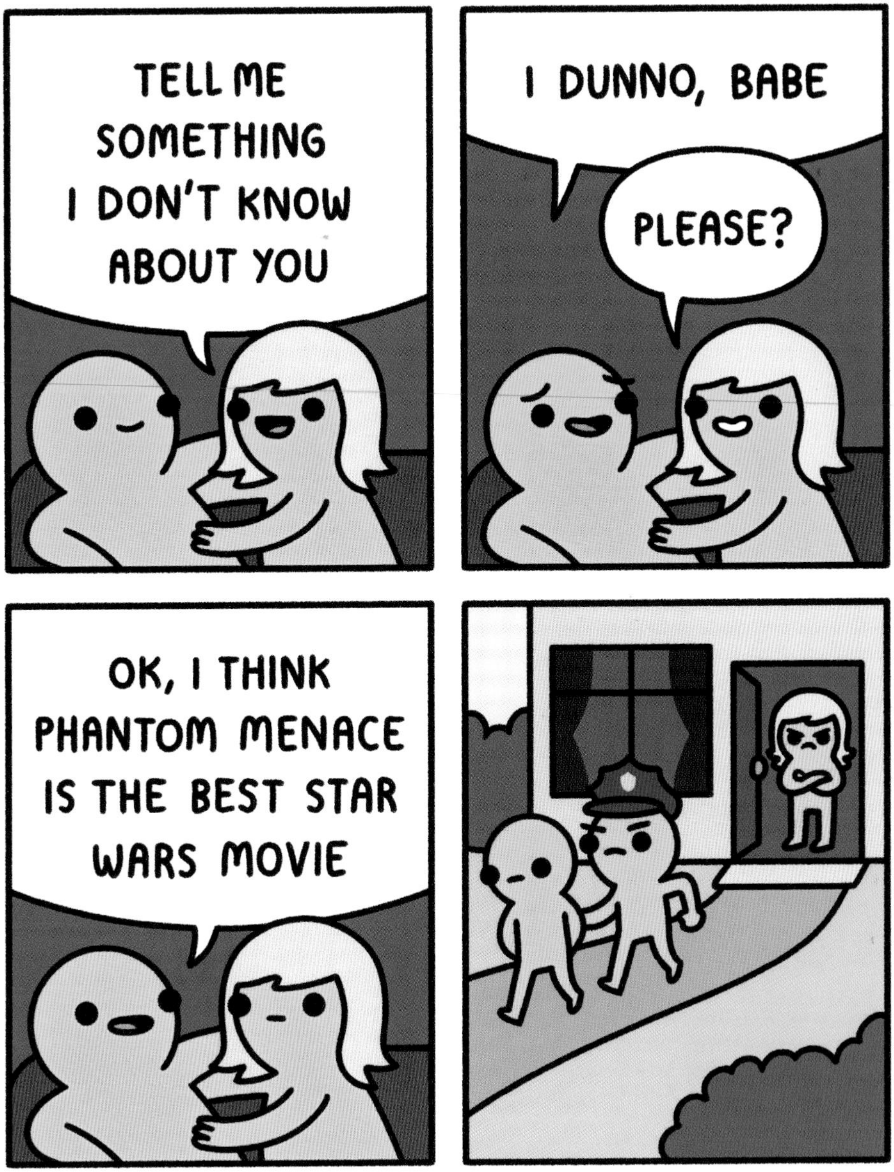
TELL ME SOMETHING I DON'T KNOW ABOUT YOU
I DUNNO, BABE
PLEASE?
OK, I THINK PHANTOM MENACE IS THE BEST STAR WARS MOVIE

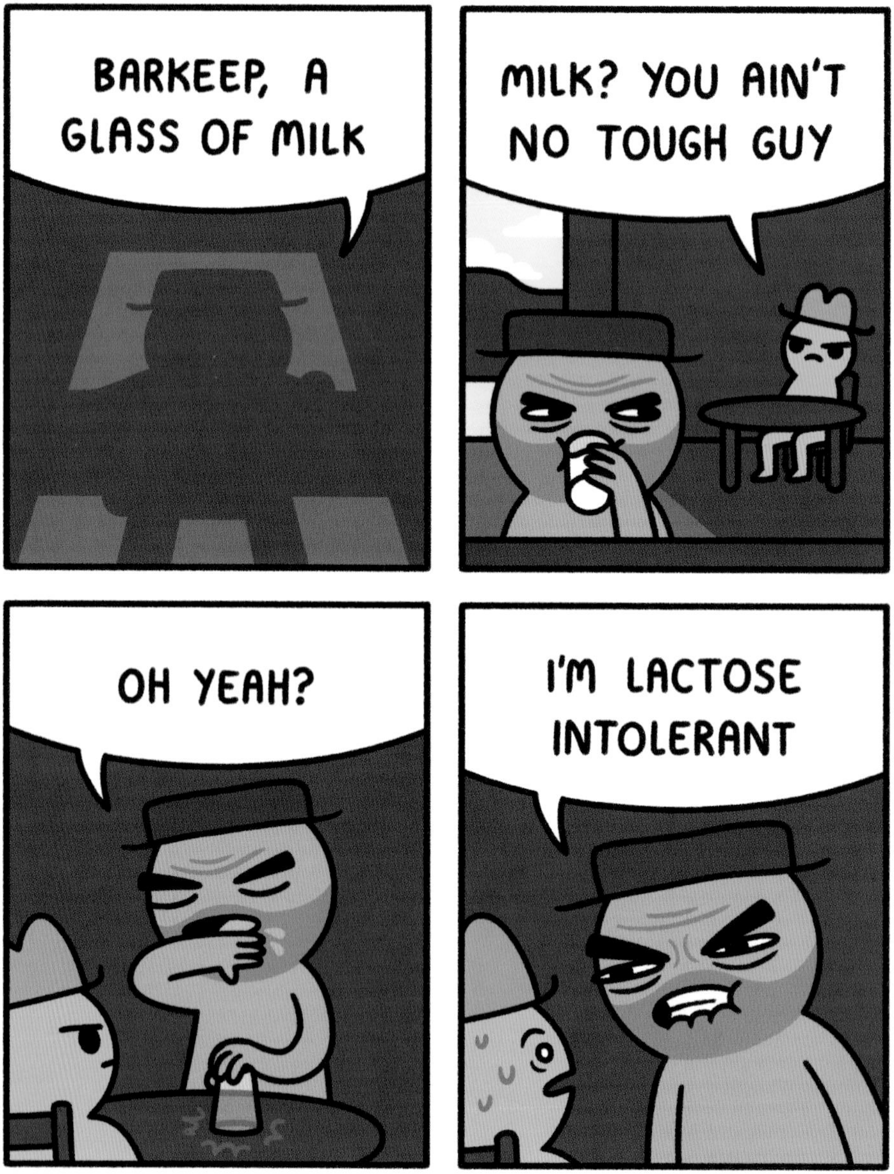
BARKEEP, A GLASS OF MILK
MILK? YOU AIN'T NO TOUGH GUY
OH YEAH?
I'M LACTOSE INTOLERANT

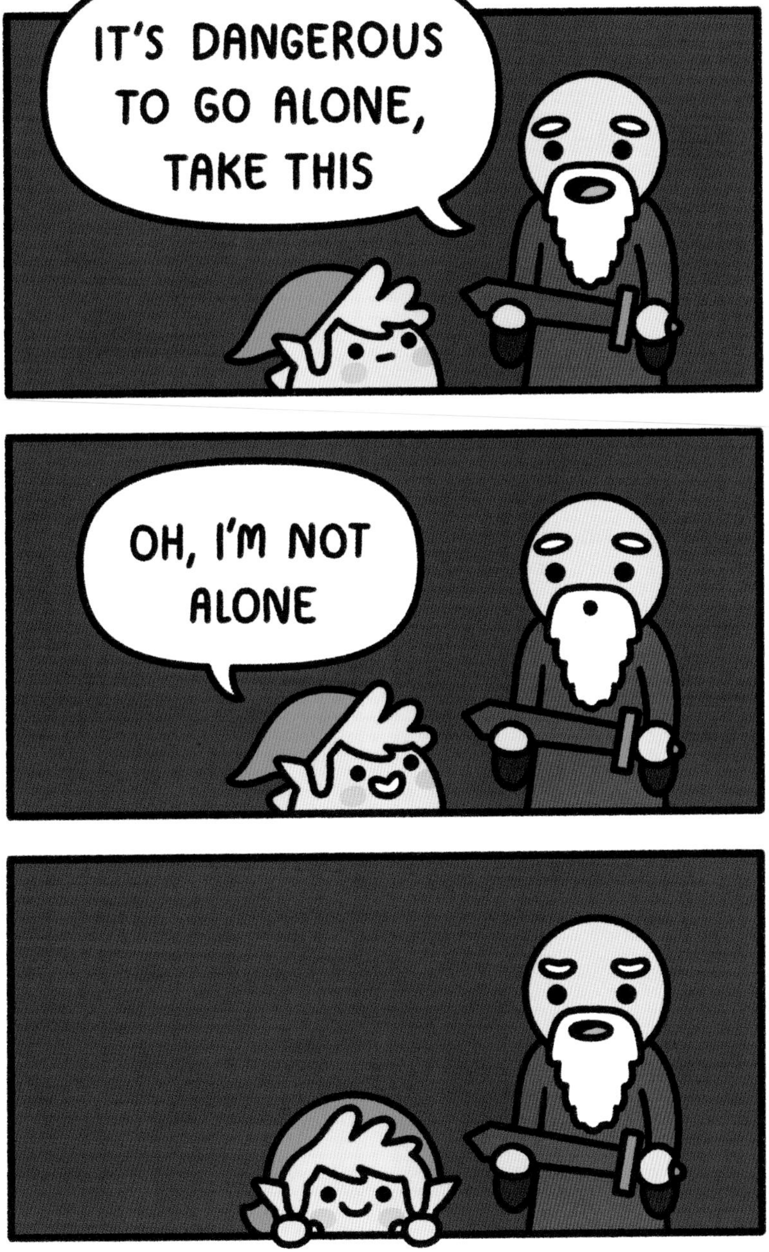
IT'S DANGEROUS TO GO ALONE, TAKE THIS
OH, I'M NOT ALONE

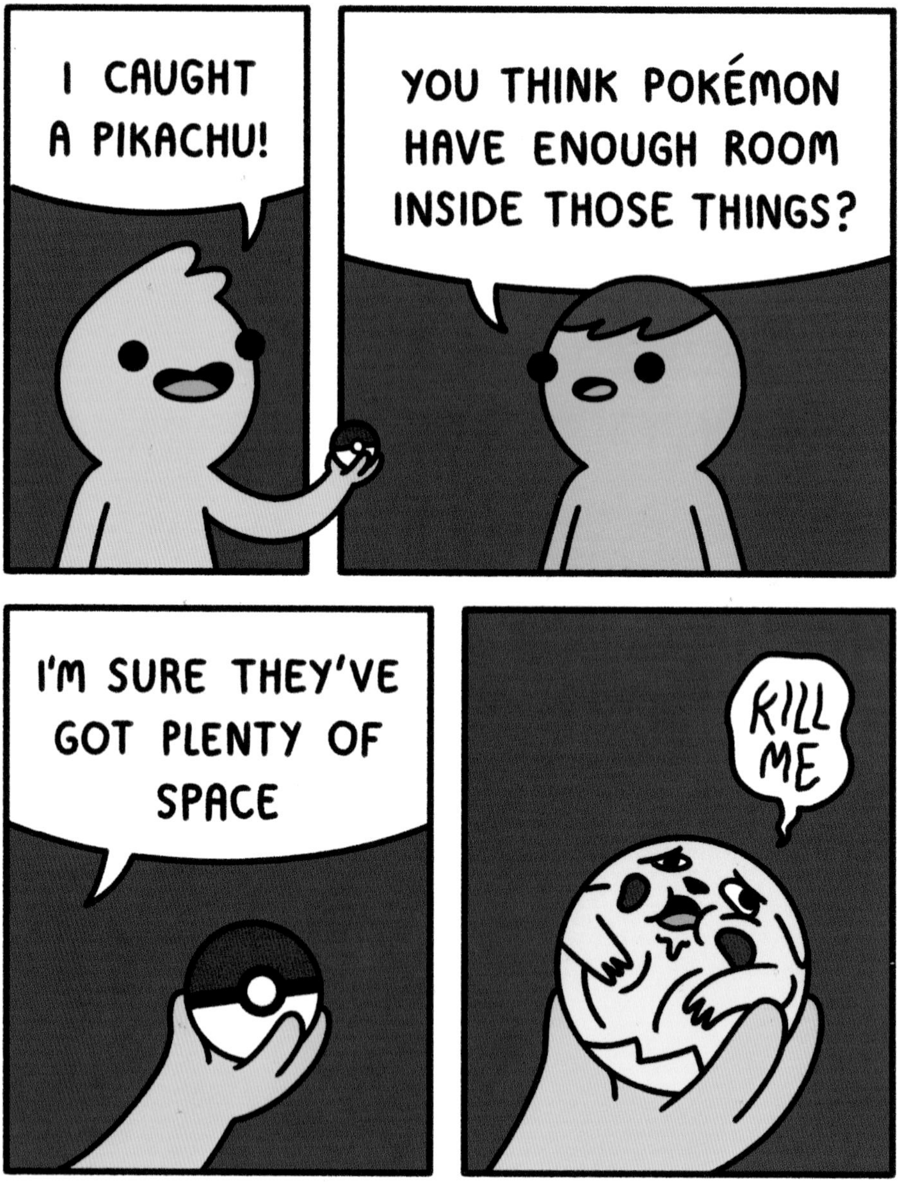
I CAUGHT A PIKACHU!
YOU THINK POKÉMON HAVE ENOUGH ROOM INSIDE THOSE THINGS?
I'M SURE THEY'VE GOT PLENTY OF SPACE
KILL ME

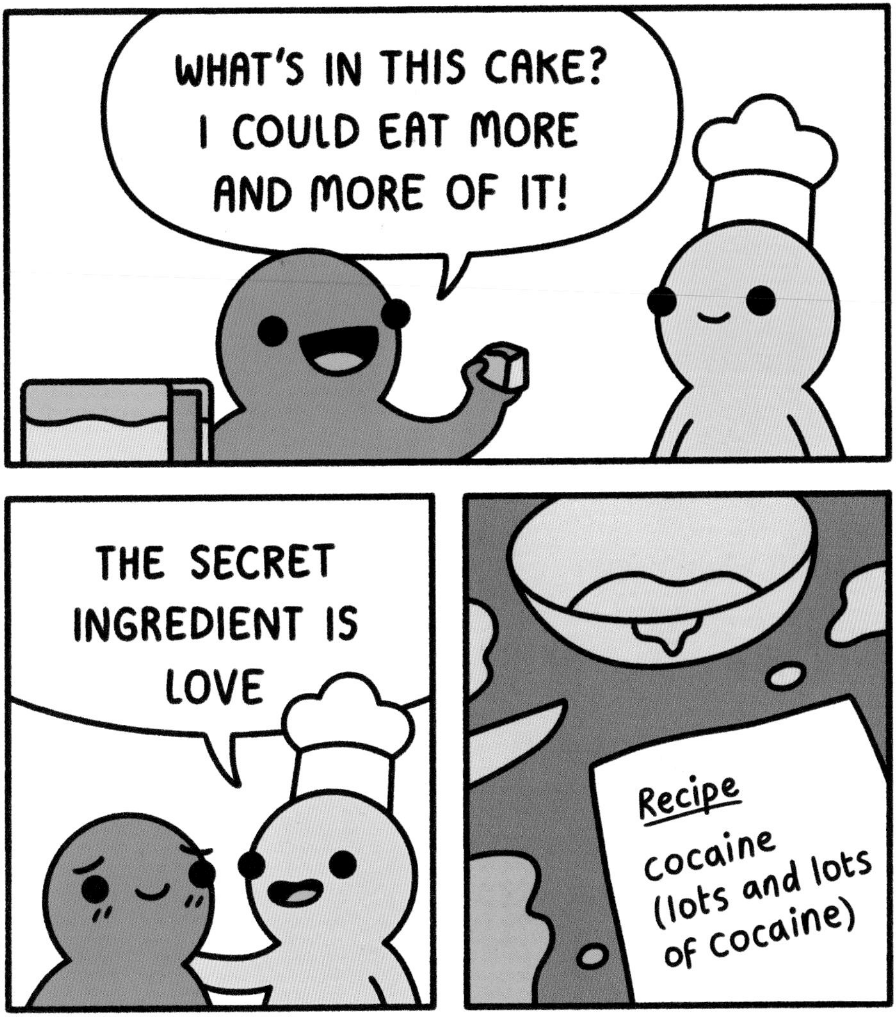
WHAT'S IN THIS CAKE? I COULD EAT MORE AND MORE OF IT!
THE SECRET INGREDIENT IS LOVE
Recipe
cocaine (lots and lots of cocaine)

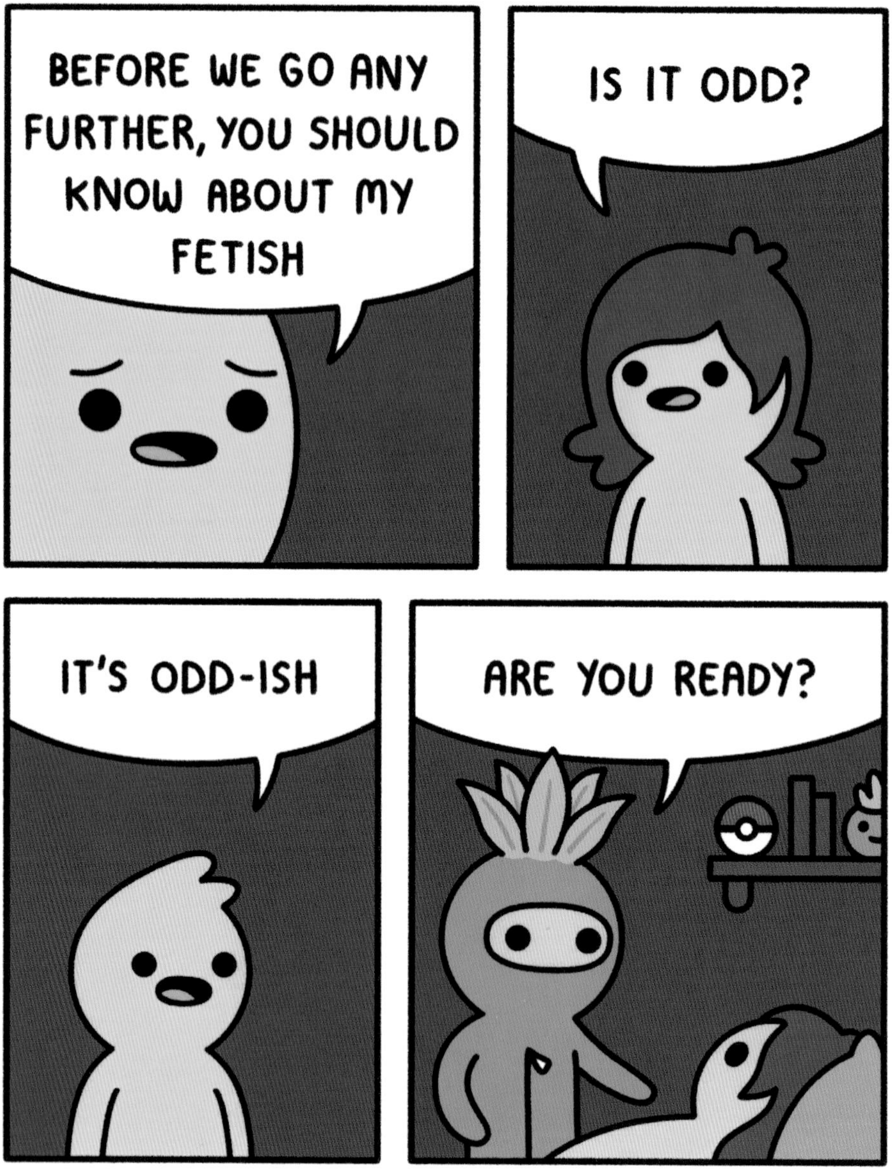
BEFORE WE GO ANY FURTHER, YOU SHOULD KNOW ABOUT MY FETISH
IS IT ODD?
IT'S ODD-ISH
ARE YOU READY?

VACUUM TOWN
ONE DAY, YOU'LL RUN THE FAMILY BUSINESS
BUT DAD... VACUUMS SUCK
THAT'S MY BOY

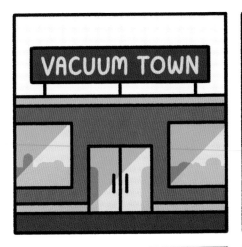

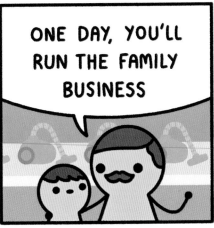

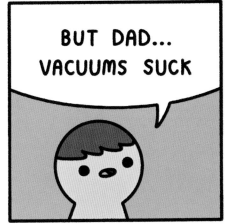

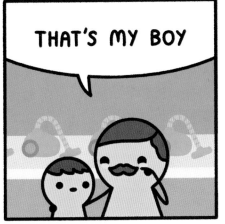

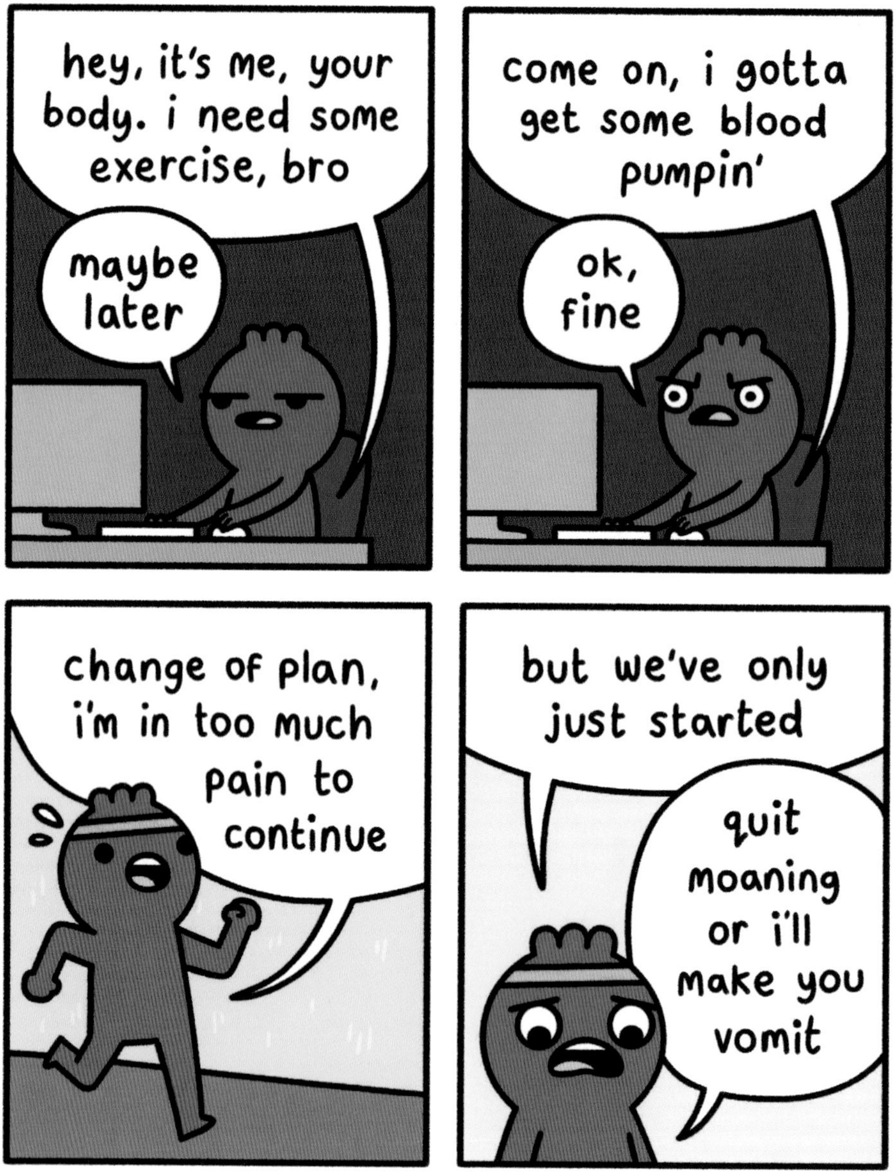
hey, it's me, your body. i need some exercise, bro
maybe later
come on, i gotta get some blood pumpin'
ok, fine
change of plan, i'm in too much pain to continue
but we've only just started
quit moaning or i'll make you vomit

WORLD 1-1
× 2
WHAT

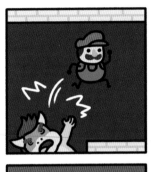

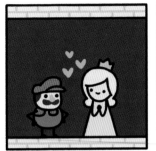

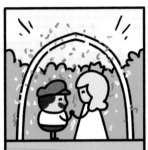

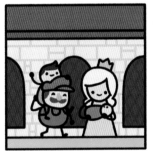

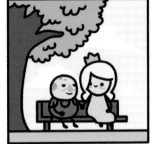

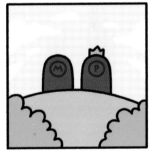

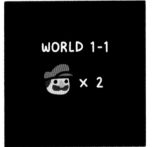

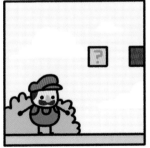

WILL YOU PUSH ME?
OK
WORK HARD IN SCHOOL
EARN THAT PROMOTION
NEVER GIVE UP ON YOUR DREAMS

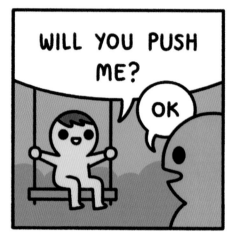

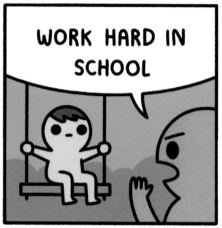

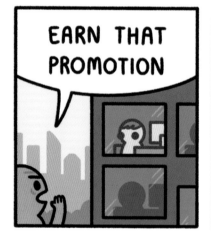

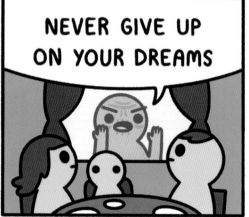

IMAGINE IF
OBJECTS COULD
TALK...

PLEASE SIT
ON MY FACE

PROBABLY
BEST NOT TO
IMAGINE

TODAY'S STEPS:
190,710
WOW... I NEED MORE EXERCISE

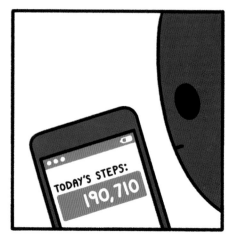

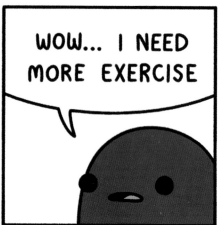

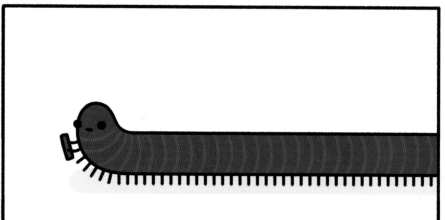

SURPRISE!
HAPPY BIRTHDAY!
OH MY GOD
I HAVE FRIENDS?

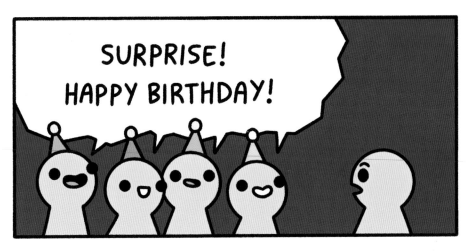

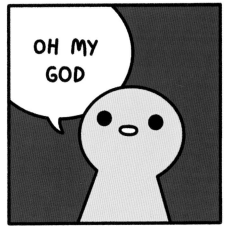

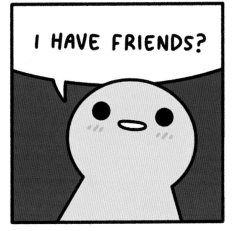

HOLY SHIT!
THE HELL WAS THAT?
Episode IV
A NEW HOPE
It is a period of civil war.
Rebel spaceships, striking
om a hidden base have wo

GO!
STARING CONTEST
#1
BOO
BOO

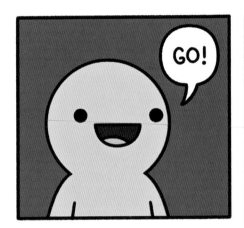

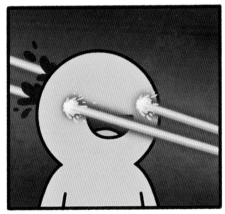

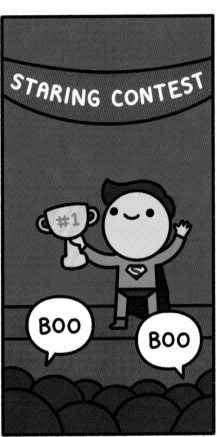

MOON

IN A RELATIONSHIP WITH EARTH

EARTH DUDE, IT WAS A ONE-TIME THING. GET OVER IT

NEPTUNE #CRINGE

MOON

IT'S COMPLICATED

PLUTO MAYBE WE COULD GRAB A DRINK SOMETIME

MOON LOL NO

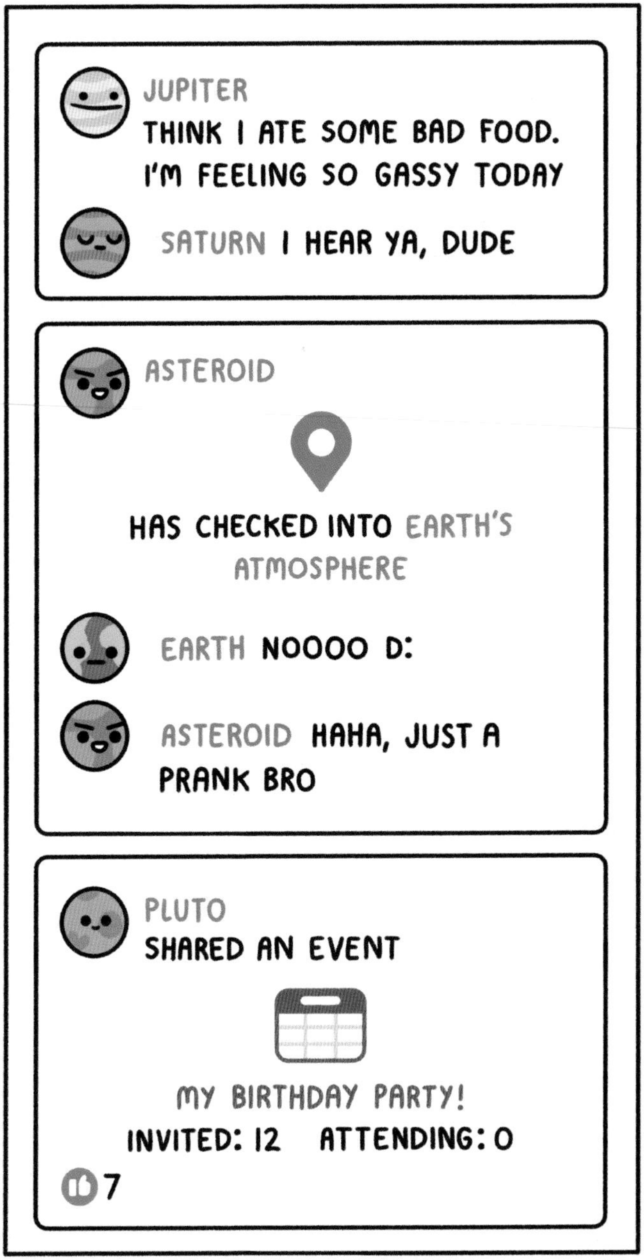
JUPITER
THINK I ATE SOME BAD FOOD. I'M FEELING SO GASSY TODAY
SATURN I HEAR YA, DUDE
ASTEROID
HAS CHECKED INTO EARTH'S ATMOSPHERE
EARTH NOOOO D:
ASTEROID HAHA, JUST A PRANK BRO
PLUTO
SHARED AN EVENT
MY BIRTHDAY PARTY!
INVITED: 12 ATTENDING: 0
7

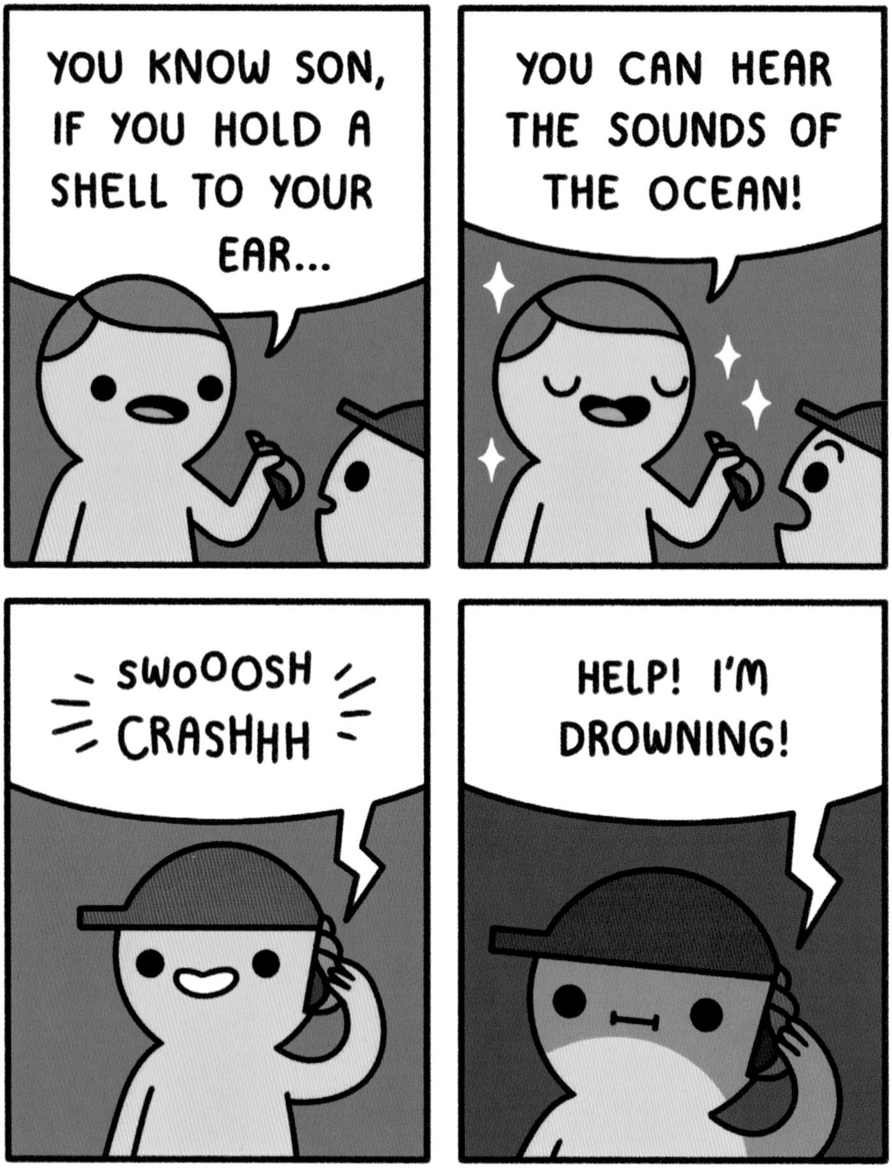
YOU KNOW SON, IF YOU HOLD A SHELL TO YOUR EAR...
YOU CAN HEAR THE SOUNDS OF THE OCEAN!
SWOOOSH CRASHHH
HELP! I'M DROWNING!

neat

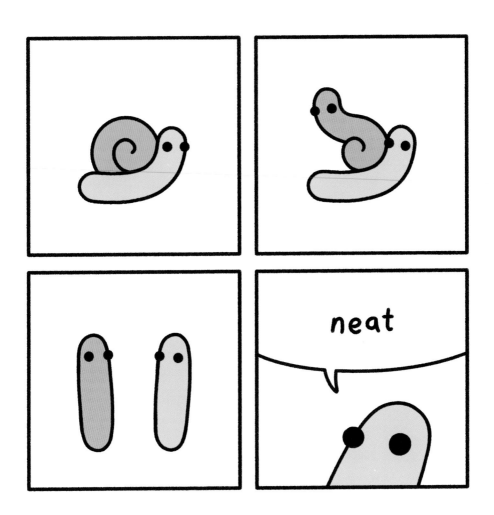

THANKS FOR READING!
SPECIAL THANKS TO WEBTOON AND MY PATREON SUPPORTERS

Andrews McMeel Publishing
a division of Andrews McMeel Universal
1130 Walnut Street, Kansas City, Missouri 64106

www.andrewsmcmeel.com

19 20 21 22 23 TEN 10 9 8 7 6 5 4 3 2 1

ISBN: 978-1-4494-9716-3

Library of Congress Control Number: 2018955954

Editor: Megan Osmundsen
Art Director/Designer: Julie Barnes
Production Editor: Amy Strassner
Production Manager: Tamara Haus
Editorial Coordinator: Lucas Wetzel

ATTENTION: SCHOOLS AND BUSINESSES
Andrews McMeel books are available at quantity discounts with bulk
purchase for educational, business, or sales promotional use. For information,
please e-mail the Andrews McMeel Publishing Special Sales Department:
specialsales@amuniversal.com.